The
Butterfly
Promise

Kristin Joy Lavin

Sunnysunshine Publishing

Author's Note
Some names have been changed to protect the identity of friends and family.
God is referred to as he or him but just in a traditional writing sense. I'm sure God is unisex and has the best of man and woman.

Author photo courtesy of Anthony Ceccarelli

Sunnysunshine Publishing

The Butterfly Promise / Kristin Joy Lavin. —1st ed.
Paperback 978-1-7351229-0-8
Hardcover 978-1-7351229-1-5
eBook 978-1-7351229-2-2

This book is dedicated to the believers and the seekers of ideas, justice and a better future for ALL of humanity.

Contents

The Promise 1

Bowling Angels 9

Me? Psychic? 13

The Dancer from Waverly Place 21

Roses in Our December 33

A Prayer with Whipped Cream on Top 39

Wine and Wafers 43

Mexican Foam 49

Everything and the Kitchen Sink 53

Sparkling Joy 63

Sprinkles 67

Italy, Ed and a lot of Gelato 81

Zippy Reincarnated? 97

Sea Monkeys 109

Tinkle of Dignity 115

Love the Soul 123

Signs 131

Erica's Psychic Gift 139

The 11:11 Phenomenon 143

On the Radio 149

Have Wings, Will Travel 151

Quantum Leap of Faith 163

THE Energy Never Dies 167

Acknowledgements 173

The Promise

I'm one in 700,000 people. Those are the odds for being a lightning victim in the U.S. in one year. I'm lucky I lived to tell the story. Am I a case study? Probably not. But my tale is rare and maybe it's given me superpowers. Probably not. But let's not rule that out yet.

I was fifteen and said goodbye to my family as I ran down the driveway toward Chrissy's parents' car. Gram called out from the front door, "Be careful Totie!" blowing me a kiss, squinting her eyes shut as her airborne peck sailed thru the air landing on my freshly washed White Rain curls.

My best friend Chrissy invited me on her family vacation to Lake George, New York, a resort community in the Adirondacks. We arrived at our cabin in the woods to sunny skies. The resort manager encouraged us to take the canoes out for a spin. We spotted the silver metal canoes lined up at the shore and chose the one closest to the dock. Neither of us had ever paddled a canoe before but we seemed to get the hang of it with a rhythm all our own. We giggled, digging our oars in and out repeatedly until we managed to be far from shore and any parents.

My propensity for the peculiar surfaced the very moment the sun disappeared under a blanket of gray clouds. With a rumble of thunder and ominous skies before us, I shrieked, "Chrissy, row back to shore, row back to shore!"

A bolt of lightning crackled across the sky. Mother Nature exhaled a gust of spiteful air, blowing my hair back.

"Lightning! We're in a metal canoe on the water. Row!" I shouted.

Panicked, we paddled but spun round and round, going nowhere. Looking over at our resort, we saw twenty people waving their arms and screaming at us.

"You row on the left, I'll row right," Chrissy shouted.

With our heads down, we coordinated our paddling and moved forward toward the shore. Another bolt of lightning and roar of thunder shook the sable sky. I felt pressure on my head and tingling in my fingers.

"Oh my God, do you smell that?" I asked.

"Burnt hair!" we both screamed.

Fearful of another strike we paddled faster in unison, making it back to shore where horrified onlookers were waiting under the drizzling skies yanking our arms, pulling us out of our canoe.

With nothing more than the terrifying ordeal and strands of singed hair, not wanting to tempt fate it took me years before I ever went back into a canoe or out in a thunderstorm.

Back at home I told everyone how I almost died, except my family. I downplayed the incident until Chrissy's mom told my mom who then told Gram.

"Totie, I love you more than life itself. If anything happened to you I would just die."

But when roles were reversed and I worried, Gram wanted me to accept her death as "part of life."

The older she got and the more real that became I had a harder time accepting one day she would die and leave me for good.

When Gram was in her mid nineties she got up to use the bathroom in her room at the nursing home. Feeling faint, she passed out hitting her eye on the doorknob of the bathroom. She was rushed to the ER where my mom Lola and I met her.

We waited two hours with Gram lying on the gurney until she was examined, X-rayed and then prepped for surgery. The ER doctor explained we needed an eye surgeon because the blood needed to be vacuumed out from behind the retina, adding that vision might be lost in her left eye. And as horrible as that was, at ninety-six years old, the bigger threat was whether she would make it through the surgery.

Lola is a nurse and told me to always ask the nurses who the best doctors are. Topping the short list of eye surgeons was Doctor Herman, a pouchy, balding, gray haired man of about fifty-five. He had a warm smile and compassionate eyes.

He came over to us just before the surgery and said, "I see how special Vivian is to you so I will take extra special care of her. If there is any chance to save the eye, I will do it. I don't give up on people just because of their age."

Neither did I.

A tall, fortyish man in blue scrubs walked in, asking for Vivian's family.

"I'm Doctor Martin, the anesthesiologist assisting Doctor Herman. I'll do my best but I can't make any promises with a head injury and her age."

As my mom remained calm and asked about which anesthesia would be used, I burst into tears. I had not shed one until the realization came about Gram not making it through the surgery. The death of Gram, my everything, was one of my greatest fears.

I either cracked through Doctor Snowmeiser's chilly shell or he suffered from intimacy issues because he quickly stammered, "I can use a mild anesthesia that's great for older folks and we'll keep her sedated for a shorter amount of time. It'll be, uh, fine."

Now that's more like it. Have some positivity man.

I didn't want lies just some reassurance then let God take it from there.

Lola and I waited in the waiting room during the surgery. I looked around at the beige walls, sat on the padded maroon chair then watched a fly buzz around the room hoping it wouldn't land on me. I hated to think where it was before here. I thought about how depressing this freaking room was. They should make hospital waiting rooms cheerier, beige and maroon are just not happy colors. My mom drank hot tea and I clasped my hands and made circles with my thumbs, the way I often do when I am in a trance-like state. CNN blared, drowning out the pages in the hallway calling for doctors and codes.

Two hours later Doctor Herman, dressed in scrubs, walked in.

"Vivian made it through fine. There is still a substantial amount of blood in the back of the eye that needs to drain on its own. That will take time. But unfortunately I can't guarantee she will have her sight when her eye heals. We'll have to give it some time."

Gram was discharged five days later with a big patch over her eye and no vision in it. Doctor Herman remained positive and attentive to Gram telling her to give the eye time to heal and the blood to clear. He always gave her hope and we loved him for that.

✶✶✶

Gram loved to read. It was the one thing that she was still able to do the same despite her age. Her mobility had decreased, her appetite dwindled, she couldn't drive anymore, her arthritis kept her from practicing calligraphy and origami, leading her to become increasingly more sedentary in the nursing home. Books became one of the links to the outside world and entertained her like old friends.

Prior to the accident, she had just completed a book on Edgar Cayce, a medical intuit practicing in the early 1900's, who diagnosed illnesses when he was in meditation. After that, the entire six-volume set of her idol, Winston Churchill's *The Second World War*. It was four thousand seven hundred and thirty-six pages.

Three months passed and the loss in her left eye seemed permanent. I was still hopeful that it would come back but she started to give up on that notion. She was depressed saying, "I'm old and decrepit."

Like a cardinal with a broken wing, she was stuck in one place unable to do what she loved most. She didn't bounce back physically or emotionally like we all assumed she would. She was able to read a few pages at a time but then her good eye would get tired and strained.

One Friday afternoon, I went over with pizza, for the two of us, like I usually did. Hoping she'd feel better today, I walked in with the warm slices and a big smile.

"Hi Gram. Pizzatime."

Normally, just visiting made her happy, but lately it had been different and I wasn't enough. I gave her a kiss, put the box down and opened it up.

"Hi, my darling Totie. Thanks, it smells good." She kissed me on the cheek and stroked my wavy brown curls.

Her room at the nursing home was cheery yellow and the horseshoe shaped alcove of windows brought in the sun. The sills had flowers and framed photos of my mom, my brother John and me. I hung two framed pictures on the wall opposite the bed. One was of famous Shakespeare quotes and the other of a beautiful giraffe, she loved them ever since I could remember.

I listened intently as a child when she explained her admiration.

"They're so regal and beautiful. Each one has its own unique pattern on its coat. They can sleep and have babies standing up."

Astonished with her mesmerizing facts and stories, I reveled in her undivided attention. I giggled and sparkled like a disco ball. I could never get enough of Gram as a kid.

As we sat there and ate, she asked, "Did you watch *The Wizard of Oz* last night?"

"Of course I did Gram. I've only seen it fifty times," I joked.

My first memory of my grandma is when I was nearly five years old and my parents and brother went to Florida. I was sick with a virus so I stayed home with Gram who lived downstairs in her own apartment.

Upstairs we had an olive green shag rug, orange couches and black leather and chrome Barcelona chairs. Very groovy. That night she brought up her old fashioned wooden rocker. It was a gift from my parents to her when she first became a grandma.

We stayed up and watched *The Wizard of Oz*. It was the first time I saw it. I sat on her lap while she rocked back and forth singing "Somewhere Over the Rainbow." Like a warm cookie in an oven, I was where I was supposed to be. Snuggled on her lap in my Wonder Woman pajamas, I watched Dorothy and Toto enter into a rainbow colored world filled with friends: a lion, a scarecrow and a tinman. When they ventured on the yellow brick road for the first time all together, Gram jumped up, turned up the volume knob, grabbed my hand and we skipped back and forth down the hallway singing "We're Off to See the Wizard." As my little brunette braids swung side to side, the shag sprung up between my toes and I howled with laughter.

The Wizard of Oz has remained my favorite movie of all time. I loved Toto so much that I became Totie to Gram for the rest of her life.

We finished our pizza and she scrunched up her face, "I don't think my sight is coming back, Totie." She turned her face toward me so she could see me out of her good eye.

"Gram, the doctor said to give it a few months," I said. Giving up on people is not in my DNA.

"What if I can't read anymore?"

Her blurred vision and headaches stopped her from reading more than a few pages in a book or an article in her *Readers Digest*. It was a slow improvement and she was impatient and discouraged with her recovery.

"Gram, even if it never came back you will still be able to read. Doctor Herman said your other eye will compensate for the loss," I assured her.

"If I can't read, I may as well be dead." She lowered her eyes and stared at the tiled floor then folded her hands in her lap.

That startled me. She was always a positive person.

"Please don't say that, Gram. You pulled through this and have come so far already. You'll get better each and every day. You will."

The bruises on the side of her face were still there, a tie-dye swirl of blues, purples and yellow. A young person's bruises would have been gone in these three months.

"Totie, I can't live forever."

"I know but I don't know what I'll do without you, Gram."

"You'll go on and be as happy as you are. You have your whole life ahead of you. And I will always be around." She stared at me intently.

"Do you promise?" My throat tightened and hurt as I spoke. I couldn't cry for me when she was the one suffering.

"Gram will always be around. We'll always be together. Forever and ever," she said with certainty. She reached for my hand and squeezed it.

"I'll send you a sign." She smiled and thought for a moment.

She let go of my hand, brushed my cheek, leaned toward me and said, "I'll send you a butterfly."

Bowling Angels

Gram moved into our house because my parents were having marital and financial problems. My dad built Gram a one-bedroom apartment downstairs in our high ranch on Long Island. The neighborhood was filled with many similar Queens transplants that longed for a better life in suburbia. Maple, oak and mimosa trees flourished in yards and the streets had black iron lampposts that mysteriously popped on at dusk making me believe in wizardry. That was the signal for all the kids to report home after hours of freely roaming around the neighborhood. Most of the houses were high and low ranches that were built in the 1960's. It was very *Edward Scissorhands* because hundreds of houses had the same basic style in either golden rod yellow, olive green (that was mine), burnt sienna, brick red, or baby blue.

Gram's apartment became my safe haven filled with sleepovers, *Donny and Marie* sing-alongs, *Love Boat* airings and afternoons of polishing Gram's silver collection with pink paste in a jar. With the escalating tension between my parents and their busy work schedule, my brother John and I spent a chunk of our childhood with Gram.

More than the fun, Gram was there for me during a time when I couldn't process the notion of my mom and dad breaking up. Gram assured me it was not my fault and they both still loved me. I believed her because for as long as I could remember, Gram was my kindred spirit. In her presence, I felt safe and could trust anything she said.

One night while my mom was in nursing school, Gram tucked me into bed after *Mork and Mindy*. An hour later I awoke to flashes of light outside my window and loud booms of thunder. I covered my head but that just made the flashing light go away, the rumbling seemed to get louder as if it was directly over my head. I wrapped myself in the blanket and ran to Gram in the living room.

"Gram, I'm scared," I cried, jumping on her lap.

"Gram is here, Totie. Don't be afraid. It's the angels in heaven. The angels are bowling." She rocked me back and forth.

"They are?" I asked, lifting my head out of her chest.

"Even angels get a night off to have fun Totie," she said patting my back.

I went back to bed when the angels finished their game.

The next day Gram had some explaining to do.

"Who are these angels? What do they do?" asking in one breath as I twirled around Gram like a planet orbiting the sun.

"The angels are spirits that guide and protect us. They are full of love and only want the best for others," she explained.

"That sounds like you Gram. Are you my angel?" stopping in mid rotation around her.

"I'll be yours and you'll be mine here on Earth. Deal?" she held out her hand for a shake.

Shaking her hand I remember thinking how lucky I was to have an angel in heaven looking out for me plus Gram right here by my side.

"Are angels people that are dead, like Clarence in *It's a Wonderful Life*?" I asked.

"I hope so Totie then my brother Percy could be an angel," she said smiling, her eyes off someplace else.

I had never known anyone that died yet but I had hoped that if I did, they would get to be an angel, flying around the world doing good deeds, helping people and God.

✳✳✳

Death is reliable and perhaps felicitous. It showed up when I was about eight.

Our neighbors, the Pelozzi family, had five children, a cat and a black Lab named Tiger who was allowed to roam free around the neighborhood, mainly because he was neglected.

One day I was walking to my friend Chrissy's house to play Candyland and listen to Olivia Newton-John's new record *Totally Hot,* when a yellow Lab ran by me, barking. I turned around and saw that Tiger was the pursuer. Their feet dashed past me on the concrete. The yellow Lab tried outsmarting Tiger and sprinted diagonally across the street. A car turned the corner, screeched on its brakes and struck the yellow Lab. The lady got out and I ran over.

"Is that your dog?" she covered her mouth with her hands.

"No," I whimpered. I walked over and knelt down beside it. The dog had vomit and blood coming out of its mouth. I started crying. The lady ran over to the house on the corner to call the police.

Looking around and spotting the neighbor's dog, "Tiger!" I screamed, "Bad dog!"

Tiger turned around and ran home while I sat on the concrete, next to the fading dog who lay there in a crimson pool spilled on the street.

I needed to stay with him.

I watched the dogs belly move up and down, his eyes flutter and his mouth twitch. As I stroked his back he never looked up. I wondered where his family was. Did they know he was hurt?

Three older boys from third grade peddled by on their Huffy bikes rubbernecking, saying,"Ewww, gross," as they rode by.

When I looked back down he was completely still. Instinctively, I knew he was dead. I had never seen anyone die but it was like Gram with the long brass candle snuffer putting out a flame. His fire was gone.

The poor doggy was no longer in pain dying on the street. I hoped he was with God and the bowling angels now and they would take care of him.

His death was more than the stepping on an ant or the squish of the fly swatter I had seen before. There was suffering, emotionally for me and physically for the dog. It ignited a wonder in me that has never left.

The transformation of life.

Me? Psychic?

I rarely remember dreams but I awoke knowing this one was pivotal in my journey of expansion.

I was lying down and looking up to the heavens, where an older, bald man was floating above me. He never said his name but I sensed he was friendly or I knew him. He seemed determined to tell me something important. As he floated in a misty cloud above me, I felt at peace, yet awake and alert. His voice was tranquil as he spoke these six words, "Tell Erica I will be OK."

I awoke and looked at the clock. It was nine, Sunday morning and I heard the birds' symphony and the faint sound of a barking dog outside my window.

My husband Joe stirred, rolled over and squinted at me, "Good morning honey."

"Good morning," I yawned and smiled at the same time. I froze in mid-stretch when I remembered the dream and wanted to tell him right away or I'd forget as usual.

"I had the weirdest dream," I recited the dream and the man's words, adding on, "I think it was Erica's dad."

Erica was Joe's cousin's wife. Jack and Erica were the lovable, can-do couple who lived a mile away from us. Erica and I became closer over the years, finding things in common. We rode our road bikes together, took pole-dancing classes, drank mojitos on the beach and had many spiritual chats. We talked about life after death, ghosts, ESP, and alien abductions. All the things that seemed hardly believable were believable to us. The crazier the better.

Erica was fun, smart, savvy and hated being petite. Her Irish-Italian roots blessed her with raven hair, a porcelain complexion, a love for food and family, and big green eyes like Madonna, the pop star. She was bubbly and had a knack for showmanship. She'd danced her whole life, first in musicals. She moonlighted as Sparkles The Clown for parties, with hundreds of screaming kids who wanted Sparkles to dance the Sparklesdance in a pink fuzzy wig and giant pink shoes.

After that, she opened a dance school. At any time, you could find her pirouetting across her living room floor with her three young daughters behind her doing the same.

I was thinking about my dream, lying in our lavender bedroom with our cats, Sprinkles and Lilly, both curled up at my feet when the phone rang. Joe jumped up and ran toward the kitchen with his boxers on, skidding down the hallway *Risky Business* style, "I'll get it."

"Hello…Oh hi Aunt Ginger. What? Oh no." Then silence.

Joe walked further down the hall where his conversation was muted. A minute later he returned and stood in the doorway of our bedroom. "Kristin, you are neva gonna believe this," his eyes were wide and mouth hung open, "Erica's dad passed away last night."

I was shocked. I barely knew Erica's dad. Why would he choose me? I decided it was because I was an open-minded person. Tell me you've had an alien encounter and I'll ask, where were they from? Tell me you bought a crystal ball and I'll ask to borrow it. It was that simple. And that complicated. I had to decide what to do. Should I tell Erica that her dad came to me in a dream? Or should I never tell for fear that she'd think I was A) Crazy B) Lying C) Weird D) All of the Above. Plus, being with a grieving person is uncomfortable. I always want to say the right thing and "I have a message from your deceased dad," may not have been the words Erica wanted to hear from me. I wasn't a medium. I half-doubted myself and the divine message I had received but in my heart I felt it meant something.

Empathy Lavin could be my alias. I imagined if my mom or Gram died and their spirit came to Erica, I would want her to tell me. She was really close to her dad and she was heartbroken when he died. Maybe this would offer her some comfort. Either that or she'd think I was a headcase and run the other way. I decided to wait until after the funeral and then feel her out.

Three weeks later, we stopped by Jack and Erica's one night. If we had a moment alone and I felt the vibe was right, I would tell her.

Joe, Jack and the kids left the kitchen table to play video games and we were alone.

She added water to the kettle, "Chamomile or Green?" she asked.

"Chamomile," I needed to soothe my nerves.

My mouth was like an old nail file, dry and useless. My heart raced as I pushed out the words, "Erica, I have to tell you something."

She turned to me, her green eyes inquisitive and inspecting.

"Erica, I know this is going to sound really weird and I wasn't even sure if I should tell you this but I feel like it's the right thing."

"Y e a h?" her voice stretched out the word. Her long black eyelashes lowered as she dropped the teabags in the mugs then came over to the table.

"Your dad contacted me in a dream the night he passed away," I blurted, thinking maybe if I said it quick it would sound better.

"Really?" Not a hint of doubt in her voice. She sat down at the table next to me.

I cleared my throat, took a deep breath and said, "He wanted me to give you a message. He told me to tell you that he is OK."

"Oh my God. That's amazing," she murmured.

She sat there stunned and smiling while I gave her every little detail of what I remembered. She hung on my every word, hugged me, then said, "That's my dad." She paused and added, "Thank you."

After that, Erica had her own contacts with her dad. They had always played this penny game. They'd spot one and say, "A penny, for a rainy day," and pocket the penny. A few days after I told her, Erica was riding her bike and talking to her dad. A few minutes later, in the street, she came to a dead stop with her bike. There were hundreds of pennies scattered in the road in front of her.

She continued to find pennies in remarkable places and had little cosmic occurrences of her own.

Erica's reaction gave me reassurance that the afterlife connection was real and had merit. The strangeness of the whole incident was dissipating like puddles on hot blacktop. I remember thinking, hmm... that was kinda cool. It was then that I began the process of taking out the para from paranormal. Still, it was the first time a deceased person contacted me so I wasn't hanging a sign on my door reading KRISTIN LAVIN - PSYCHIC MEDIUM, anytime soon.

So what should I do with this new talent of mediumship? Why was it given to me? I had always believed that we all had a purpose here on Earth so this latest psychic experience unfolding was making me more curious at what my abilities were and tapping into them. Did I have control over them? Were they random?

The others felt trivial compared to Erica's.

Years before, I was walking in the parking lot of Target and looked up at the big red bull's-eye sign. My memory kicked in and I remembered the dream I'd had the night before. I dreamt I was in line at Target and saw an old college friend of mine named Jim.

The last time I saw Jim was the summer after college graduation. We went to the Hamptons to party and celebrate. He picked me up in his Buick and we went to an outdoor summer bar where Ace of Base was crackling from the speakers and the drinks were flowing.

A few drinks plus a lemon drop shot later, I slurred, "I gotta leave."

It was 1:30 a.m. and I was toasted. He had stopped drinking a while ago and agreed, "OK cool, let's go."

I wobbled my way across the dim parking lot and got into his car. I sat there for a few minutes. I wondered, where's Jim? He was right behind me. I started nosing around the car when I spotted loads of empty Miller cans on the floor. We never drank Miller... No way, someone broke into his car and left their empty cans... How rude. I sniffed... a pungent Vanillaroma air freshener?.....huh? Just then I spotted Jim outside my window in hysterics.

I was in someone else's car.

That was the last time I saw Jim. We got caught up in our summer jobs, other friends and eventually lost contact. So when he popped into my dream, I was shocked because I hadn't thought about him in several years.

I walked through the swinging glass doors of Target and grabbed a cart. I shopped around and forgot about my dream. I picked up a sunhat, a No Doubt CD, a notepad and a few other odds and ends made in a third world country that I really didn't need.

I was waiting in line when I looked over and standing a few lines away was Jim. I had sunglasses on so we didn't make direct eye contact but I think he saw me.

I never said a word to Jim that day. I was in shock and didn't know what to say. I kept thinking: this is so weird over and over in my head. I was so focused on my ESP experience, the moment passed and was gone forever.

Shortly after that one, involved psychic medium, John Edward. I was walking down Main Street, meeting Joe for Greek food. Strolling toward the restaurant, I had a fleeting image of running into John Edward. His round face appeared in my head, staring at me with piercing blue eyes. I looked around and no one familiar was in sight so I shrugged it off as silly and kept my pace, knowing pitas and hummus were definitely in my future. I had learned who he was from *Sixty Minutes,* where he was channeling spirits for money and ballroom dancing for fun. He wasn't that famous yet.

Over dinner I told Joe about the wacky feeling and we laughed. We went home that night never seeing the ghost whisperer.

The following evening we headed into town once again, this time to go for ice cream. There were no parking spaces so Joe parked illegally and waited in the car, putting in his order, "I'll have mint chip." And off I went.

I was mentally deciding what flavor I was in the mood for, mint chip, chocolate peanut butter or vanilla swiss almond, when I opened the glass door and there stood John Edward at the counter ordering ice cream.

I ran back to the car and swung the door open, startling Joe.

"You are never going to guess who is getting ice cream right this very minute!" I yelled out, ambushing him

"Where's the ice cream?"

"Skip the ice cream for a minute! John Edward!" I shrieked. "I'm going back. I have to think of what to say," I slammed the door and left Joe sitting there speechless.

On the way back I thought of all the clever things I could say. Umm… are you John Edward? No…. I knew you'd be here. Nah, better yet… I think you are supposed to tell me something. Yes that was it. That was my line. He must need to tell me something.

I walked up and opened the door.

He was gone.

Crap. I was disappointed but I was getting better at this. At least that time I was prepared to say something.

Maybe all that was in preparation to lead up to Erica's dad's psychic appearance. Like an unclenching fist, I was opening up. If it had been my first, maybe I would have never said a word, too weirded out by the experience. I considered the few before cosmic confidence builders.

Now that my antenna was up, maybe a visit to a psychic would be interesting. I imagined it would be a safe zone where I could ask questions about all these other worldly happenings. Her answers would be a soft pillow I could lay my head on.

Regardless of the occasional doubts that sprung up on me, the message felt authentic and I delivered it from a genuine place of love. Erica had confirmation her dad was OK and was undeniably happy with that. Mediums charge top dollar to give people messages. Erica's was free, not even a penny.

The Dancer from Waverly Place

"Do you wanna come over for a psychic party?" asked my sister in law Deirdre. Six girls would each receive a private one on one session with a psychic. I had never been to one - purposely. I used to think it was freaky and unnatural to know the future.

I was afraid they would tell me something bad like, "So and so will drop dead" or "Gurrrl, you're doomed." I thought it would make me second-guess my decisions and worry about my loved ones because of my protective nature.

Curiosity got the better of me and I changed my mind after I had been getting a few cosmic vibes of my own. The next time I was approached about a psychic reading I would say yes to the crystal ball.

I have always had a fascination with death, afterlife, ESP and all things spooky or spiritual - sometimes bordering on the morbid side. In college I chose my final paper on the death penalty and all the varieties offered on the menu by the states. My English term paper was on Emily Dickinson and her preoccupation with expiration. Once I was finally on board the Psychic Express, I promised myself I wouldn't live my life according to Esmeralda and what she saw in her crystal ball. I'd just do it for fun.

Call it synchronicity, *The Secret*, the law of attraction or cosmic intervention, but there I was sitting in Deirdre's cramped bedroom one year later on Long Island, face to face with a psychic lady named Susan. Yes, Susan. I hate to take the drama and mystique out of the story, but Susan was a fifty-year-old lady in stonewashed jeans and a J.C. Penney T-shirt with a bad perm. She was from Queens, New York, who did this gig on the side along with babysitting her grandchildren. She had frosty blonde highlights in her frizzy, short hair and a thick Queens accent that welcomed me, "How are ya hon?"

We sat face to face, on opposite ends of a folding table with Tarot cards dividing us. They were twice the size of playing cards and had a variety of mystical images on one side, which Susan interpreted as she flipped them over one by one. She warned me she is usually right about the prediction but her timing is sometimes off because she may interpret a three as three months, but it may be three years or even March, the third month.

Initially, she told me I'd leave my job in four months over a dispute, my husband would buy something really big and then some general things about my personality, like I hate not being liked.

Hmm, kinda generic, not that crystal ball-ish.

There were two cards left unread.

She took a deep breath, closed her painted blue eyelids and placed her long, boney fingers on the top card, flipped it over, and put it down on the table. She studied the image, closed her eyes and paused.

"An older woman figure in your life... your grandmother... will pass in four months from high blood pressure," she said.

I was completely shocked. I was always told they never tell you anything bad. Instantly sick to my stomach, I felt the sting in my eyes and a lump in my throat. I tried not to cry but the harder I tried, the more tears came out until I was eventually sobbing.

"I'm sorry sweetie but I have to give you all the information that is given to me." Susan looked genuinely sympathetic.

My grandma did have high blood pressure but she certainly wasn't at death's door. I didn't take this prediction lightly because at the age of ninety-three it was possible. And devastating for me. Any thought of Gram not being around froze me with fear.

There was one card left on the table. Please let it be a good one. I was still dabbing my tears with a tissue as she turned over the final card. She took a deep breath, opened her eyes and smiled at me, "She will be greeted in heaven by her brothers and the love of her life."

✳✳✳

Gram was born in New York City in 1911 as Estelle Vivian Mead; everyone called her Vivian because her mom was Estelle too. She was born on Waverly Place in downtown Greenwich Village. She told me there were still horse drawn carriages and men who would come around at dusk to light the gas powered street lamps when she was little.

Vivian was a brunette with porcelain skin and fine English features. If you asked Gram about her looks, the first thing she'd say was that she had "awful buckteeth" that made her self-conscious until she got them fixed in her twenties. The second thing would be that she loved to dance, especially ballet.

After Susan's prediction I wanted to have the story of Gram's life, in her own words, so she was retelling pivotal moments to me on video. After she was gone I would be able to watch the tapes, see her face and hear her voice, something she longed for with her own family.

She was self-conscious about being filmed so I asked her to talk to me and forget the camera was there, placing it on a tri-pod behind me.

Her mother Estelle was American of Irish and English descent and her father George was an immigrant from England who came over to fulfill the American Dream. George was the first in the area to sell movie ticket stub machines to movie theaters during Hollywood's Golden Age of Film.

George and Estelle's marriage was not a loving one.

"They weren't a good match," Gram said.

When Gram was a baby, her father George went back to England as he often did. He somehow obtained a return ticket back to New York in April 1912 on the maiden voyage of the Titanic.

The news of the sinking ship broke and since Estelle had not heard from George, she assumed George was killed on the Titanic. Many days later, there was a knock at the door. It was George. Estelle thought she had seen a ghost.

George got plastered the night before the ship's departure, slept late and missed the boat. He returned to New York a week later, never contacting Estelle to let her know he wasn't dead. Gram said her mother told the story with a twinkle in her eye as if to say, "too bad."

Her parents' loveless marriage made Gram desire a true love to share her life with. George came and went as he pleased while Gram and her three brothers Buddy, Percy and the youngest Clifford adored their savvy mother who was wheeling and dealing real estate in New York's Greenwich Village neighborhood. They moved three times on the same block due to her property investments.

"When I was five, we were playing ball on the sidewalk, outside our brownstone. It was still the days of horse and carriage although a few rich men had automobiles. The ball rolled into the street and my brother Clifford ran to get it. He didn't look because normally you would hear the horse and carriage coming a mile away. A wealthy man who had just purchased his first automobile was driving by and struck Clifford. He died right there on Waverly Place, in front of us," Gram told me.

"Did you understand he died Gram?"

She sighed, "Oh yes, he was my playmate. One day we were playing, the next day he was gone."

She was young but she remembered vividly the pain her mother felt and how sad her house was for years after.

"We hung a crepe on the door directly after his death. Crepes were flowers that signified a death in the family to the neighbors. My mother was in deep mourning and wore black for years. The whole family was. I wore a black bow in my hair for a year and my brothers wore black armbands over their clothes."

The family received one hundred dollars for Clifford's death from the rich man. According to the U.S. inflation calculator, that is about two thousand dollars in today's economy.

During my video sessions with Gram, I made a pilgrimage to Waverly Place. I wanted to go there while Gram was still alive so I could return with a full report and photos. She loved the idea.

I took the subway to West 4th Street and walked away from Sixth Avenue toward Washington Square Park. As I walked away from the bustle of Sixth, the streets narrowed and became curvy. They were confusing here, unlike the other side of Sixth where they ran north/south in more of a grid, but that gives it more of the neighborhood feel that people crave in a big city like New York. I continued walking west toward the Hudson River, passing old brick apartment buildings that were refurbished. Back in the day, many of the townhouses in Greenwich Village had stables connected for their horses. As cars became more common, the stables were turned into housing but you can still spot them today by their arc shaped doors and shorter ceilings.

Gram's neighborhood became a historic district back in the 1970's because some of buildings dated back to 1799. Now, most of the buildings on Waverly were residential with a few exceptions like the dry cleaner and a sweet little bookstore on the corner.

I followed the addresses as the numbers went up until I found the brownstone where she was born. The building next door had a marker on it that read 1838. Hers was a rusty color outside with a few steps leading up to a black metal door. It was a few stories high and I imagined had quite a view of the community's mixture of architecture.

I stood on the sidewalk listening to a bird's incessant chirping despite only a few trees lining the sidewalks. I slowly spun around looking at the mixture of brownstones and red brick buildings with wrought iron bannisters and fire escapes, imagining Gram back in the day running off to dance class with her size five pink toe shoes hanging from satin strings in her hand. She'd pass women in large, feathery hats and petticoats and men in bowler and top hats with the loud clip-clop of horse hoofs and an occasional car echoing around her.

She'd wave and smile, careful not to show her buckteeth, at her neighbors, a mix of Irish, Italian and English, who settled in this neighborhood wedged between the Hudson and the East Rivers.

On her way, she'd walk past artists' studios, tearooms, writing spaces, fifteen-cent spaghetti restaurants and later, 1920's speakeasies. After class, where she studied tap, ballet and soft shoe, she'd catch a fifteen-cent silent movie starring one of the greats like Charlie Chaplin or her favorite leading lady Mary Pickford.

Happy and tired after a busy day, she'd arrive home where the icebox delivery was being unloaded. Her mother paid the delivery man in the crispy, white uniform twenty-five cents who handed Gram an ice chip to suck on. That delivery would keep everything cold for days.

"Hello Mother, where's Snookie?" she'd ask as she threw off her high button shoes before stomping off to find her brother Percy, not waiting for her mother's response.

Next to Snookie, she'd sit by the crystal radio and listen to the nightly broadcast of *The Happiness Boys* or *The A&P Gypsies*, musical radio shows popular in the 1920's. When the shows ended, Gram said her prayers and went to sleep.

Standing on the corner of Waverly, it was easy to see where Gram's initial love of the arts came from. Known as the Bohemian section from 1900 until 1929, Greenwich Village was a place of art, acceptance and radicalism.

By her high school years, she developed into quite a tap and ballet dancer. Petite, at a little over five feet, she made the perfect ballerina. By then she had also picked up her avid reading habit, gobbling up the classics by

Shakespeare, reading the moderns like *The Great Gatsby* and discovering what would be one of her passions, poetry.

"Dancing was my real passion. I used to love to slip on toe shoes and dance on pointe. I went to dance class every week and practiced in the house all the time," she reminisced.

In her teens, she began dancing in local community theater groups and shows. With that experience came the revelation that she wasn't going to be a kept woman. Her intention was to find a partner in life with the same fondness of art, theater, and the greats like F. Scott Fitzgerald, Robert Frost, and T.S. Elliot. The plan was to be happy and in love and she thought it was possible. It was 1928, after all.

When Gram was in her early twenties, she met a boy named Joe Z. at the community center in Queens, where her family had relocated after she graduated high school. He was tall with big, brown eyes, a square jaw, full lips and slicked back, brown hair. Movie star handsome; I've seen the pictures.

"Joe and I were instantly in love. He had a love for the arts and was very romantic. He sent me love letters and poems and drew me beautiful pictures, signing them 'As Ever, Joe.' We dressed up and went to local dances where we did the Lindy. New York was an exciting time in the 1930's. It was after prohibition and before the war and I felt free. I felt like anything was possible."

He was front and center at Gram's shows. In a program I have of hers from 1933, he wrote, "To Vivian From Joe, Who Did See A Dream Dancing."

"It was the happiest time of my life," she said, smiling as her eyes twinkled.

I wished I had even more details, but this was a part of her life she didn't relive in great detail. She held those memories in a space locked away for no one to know but her and Joe. They were private. And bittersweet.

"I suppose all good things come to an end. Joe's family was strict Catholic and did not approve of my Episcopal upbringing so Joe broke it off," Gram frowned.

"That's not fair Gram," I protested, as if I could change the past.

"Totie, it was very common at that time. People married within their own religions and ethnic backgrounds and that was that. I was heartbroken, though. I never got over Joe. We were soul-mates, as you kids say," she giggled and adjusted the little, pink chiffon scarf around her neck. It was last year's Easter present from me. Pink was her favorite color.

After the breakup, she hid her despair and kept busy with a job as a receptionist, which also helped to pay for dance lessons. She danced on weekends; tapping and pirouetting away in local musical reviews, "The Sunnyside Minstrels" and "Bird Sisters Miniature Musical Review." It was during this time, Gram became a fan of Fred Astaire after seeing him in classics, *Flying Down to Rio* and *Top Hat*.

One night, while performing on stage at the Elks Club, she met Ben.

Dressed in a double-breasted pinstriped suit and fedora, he sauntered over, took off his hat and said, "I recognize you. You were on the cover of the *Long Island Sunday Press* last week."

She was pictured on stage in an Elks performance with other ladies and then by herself on an inner page. The photo was alerting readers about daylight savings.

She showed me that photo for the first time a few years ago. It cracked me up because she continued to surprise me with all these little gems from her past. She was sitting in a clock and her legs were outstretched as the arms telling time. She was rocking high-heeled shoes and a maillot. The photo was black and white but Gram was like an iridescent rainbow popping out of a dark sky, full of hope and promise.

Even though I instantly recognized her, I still asked incredulously, "That's you?" I hadn't realized that Gram was written up in local papers until then because she never bragged.

"None other than dear old Gram," she answered.

Gram turned Ben down but her lack of interest made him even more interested, pursuing her with flowers and gifts until she caved and they started dating a few weeks later.

"He was very persistent and did have a certain amount of charm," she told me.

"He was a snappy dresser with a muscular build and nice hair. And after I had sworn off fellows for a while, it was nice to get a little attention, I suppose."

Ben was quite the party boy. Social and gregarious, he'd buy the whole bar a drink. From a German-American family in Queens, he worked in the Brooklyn Navy Yard as a mechanic after serving in the U.S. Navy. He was adored by his family and had many friends. He was the complete opposite of Joe, who was artsy, soul bearing and serious.

She rebounded with Ben and in 1936 they married, with brothers Percy and Buddy by her side. Four years later Gram gave birth to my mom, Lois.

But within a few years, Gram became increasingly unhappy in her marriage.

"I wasn't in love with him and we had very little in common," she said matter-of-factly.

She confided in Percy, her closest brother and best friend.

Snookie was handsome and always well dressed. He kept his wavy, brown hair slicked and parted to the side. He worked at a radio station in New York.

"We were so proud of that. Percy operated the equipment and often went on special news assignments," she said smiling and clasping her hands together looking directly at the lens. Gram lit up the camera as she talked about Percy.

By 1939 eighty percent of households owned their own radio and its popularity was at an all-time high. In 1938 Orson Welles hosted a radio show, which broadcast *War of the Worlds*. Over one million listeners mistook it as a newscast and panicked because they thought the world was being invaded by Martians. The power of the media was huge even back then.

One of Percy's last assignments was in February 1942, when France's ocean liner Normandie caught fire on Pier 88 in New York. After France surrendered to Germany in 1940, the ship had been held at a New York dock under protective custody. It was being converted from a luxurious ocean liner into a military ship for WWII. It was the story of a lifetime for Percy because everyone initially thought it was enemy sabotage, so news people flocked to the scene. The fire was later determined to be a spark from a welder working on board during the conversion.

Shortly after the Normandie disaster, Percy became ill. The infection traveled to his kidneys and on April 24, 1942 Percy died of kidney failure.

"I was completely devastated after his death. I would have given him one of my kidneys if I could have at the time," Gram still grieved.

She also lived with the regret of never getting to say goodbye.

"At the hospital, his wife was too afraid to be with him at the end and they wouldn't allow me to go in the room. I stood outside in the hallway while my brother died alone," Grams eyes glassed up, then blinking a few times to dry them up.

Photos of the inferno appeared the following year in an issue of *Coronet* magazine. Gram and her mom, Estelle were flipping through the magazine and discovered a now deceased Percy standing next to New York City Mayor Fiorello LaGuardia, with the ship in flames in the backdrop. Clutching the magazine to her chest, Estelle grabbed Gram's hand and wept for her second fallen son.

I have known about Percy for as long as I can remember. Percy this and Percy that. I never realized until I got older that he died so young because Gram kept him alive with her stories, her memories and her love. She never let him die.

With Percy gone she reflected on her own life and knew she'd made mistakes. The same year Percy died, she separated from Ben and became a single mom in 1942.

"Why Pop-Pop Gram? Why did you get married in the first place?" I asked, zooming in the camera.

She rolled her eyes and snorted, "Ugh, I don't know what I was thinking Totie!"

She paused thoughtfully "… he was different and he was kind. He even saved up money and fixed my buckteeth. But we had nothing in common."

He wanted to make her happy because he really did adore Gram.

"There's always one who is the lover and the other is the beloved," repeating to me one of Gram's famous quotes.

Ouch. But true. "Well if you didn't marry Pop-Pop, I wouldn't be sitting here," I said, sugarcoating her sorrow.

"That's very true, Totie. I don't know what I'd do if I didn't have you."

"There's a Divine Order of things Gram. Life is exactly as it should be in any given moment. Mistakes included."

"However did I get such a wise granddaughter?" she said as we both laughed.

My grandma had a boyfriend or two over the years but Joe was the true love of her life and she found it difficult to bounce back after losing him. To make matters more challenging, Ben wouldn't give Gram a divorce because divorces were only granted due to three reasons in the 1940's: cruelty, desertion and adultery. Marriage was considered a sacred bond to be protected by church and state. Since none of the three were accurate, Gram and Ben remained married for several years until Gram heard about "quickie divorces" in Juarez, Mexico. My mom's first plane ride was to El Paso, Texas with Gram during a one-day round trip to the Mexican border where Gram obtained a divorce from Ben, so they could both move on with their lives.

Gram spent the time after Percy's death driving the Red Cross vehicle and delivering blood donations during the end of the war. After the war she worked as a secretary and focused her energy on her aging parents and raising my mom, Lois. She gave up on her dreams of dancing.

Around 1955, she married Larry, her second husband. They had a short but happy marriage. He passed away around 1960. Gram never remarried again.

Gram continued, "My brother, Buddy passed away on April 24, 1990. Buddy always told the family for years that he thought he would die on the same day as our brother Percy. He did, forty-eight years later to the date. Can you imagine?" she paused. "Your mom and I attended the funeral on Long Island and Buddy's wife put a notice in *Newsday*. A few days later, my phone rang and a man asked, 'Hello, is this Vivian Mead?' So I said, 'Well I was Vivian Mead, who is this?' I hadn't used my maiden name in years so I thought that was a bit strange. Then the man said 'I have been looking for you for years, Vivian. It's Joe…. Joe Z.'"

Roses in Our December

"How did you find me?" Gram gripped the phone receiver turning her knuckles white.

"I saw your name in your brother Buddy's obituary," Joe replied.

Joe was widowed years before. Scouring newspapers and phone books, he had searched for Gram for years. She was seventy-nine when Joe called, ending their fifty-year estrangement.

Gram covered her flushed cheeks with her frail little hands, "I couldn't believe it Totie. The love of my life found me after all those years! He never forgot me either."

Even though it was incredible that Joe looked her up over fifty years later, I wasn't all that shocked. Beautiful in and out, my grandma left an impression on everyone she met. Still graced with smooth, glowing skin, she didn't look her age claiming it was all the Vaseline she used. We have the same heart shaped face and people often said that I looked like her. With my high cheekbones, darker complexion and brown eyes, I had the exotic look while she looked aristocratic. I didn't see our resemblance but considered it a compliment.

Still, Gram was concerned with seeing Joe again after all these years. At seventy-nine and a fifty-plus-year absence, that would make any woman feel a bit insecure.

Joe began sending her love letters with poems about lost love. "We remember youth's sweet April's fragrant season; knowing hour glass sands have but one reason. Those grains in the glass, tell of a long ago past; and the bottom seems to be filling too fast. We both remembered; we must not forget."

"I was nervous but I decided to send Joe a recent photo so I put a warning on the envelope; 'Wear rose colored glasses before opening.' He wrote back, 'I took my chances by not heeding the warning, nor did I require them after opening. Now everything all around has taken on a rose-colored hue!'" Gram told me.

He sent her a recent photo back with a letter that said, "Now that I have found you, I must calm my impatience with writing often. Looking at a 1944 photo and my reflection in the mirror, I realized that a unique circumstance exists for us in reverse. We must first forget to remember the old us and get to know the new us and for a while that can only be done by writing."

"Did you recognize Joe in the photo he sent?" I asked.

"Yes and he was still a handsome devil." Typical Gram reply.

Three months passed along with many letters back and forth, getting reacquainted. Two sets of plans were made, Gram canceled the first, Joe the second, both claiming maladies. Gram made a decision.

"Let's remember each other the way we were," Gram said to Joe, he agreed.

The pen was a shroud obscuring their age and the painful past. Written words offered security and agelessness, rhythmically picking up where they left off many years ago. Joe lived only twenty-five minutes away from my mom's house, where Gram had her apartment. It wasn't the distance that kept them apart just the distance of the years that had gone by.

Along with love letters, they caught up on the phone a few times a week discussing their families and news, debating, just as before, politics, world affairs and literature.

I really wished they had seen each other but both were strong-willed, that never changed. My mom and I both offered to drive Gram to meet Joe but she always declined. The last time I asked, she answered me with a Shakespeare quote, "Totie, 'Love looks not with the eyes but with the mind.'"

In other words, stop asking.

They only saw each other once since their split fifty years prior. She heard he married and moved on. He heard of her whereabouts just after their break-up but never contacted her.

Instead chance stepped in.

It was in the 1940's, shortly after World War II, fresh off her stint as a Red Cross driver for the blood delivery truck. Gram was shopping in Queens when she was tapped on the shoulder and there he was. There was some small talk and at the end of the conversation he leaned in and said, "Do you still have the last painting I gave you?"

And Gram, not wanting to act like the broken hearted women she was inside, casually replied, "It's been ten years but hmm, I think I still have it somewhere."

"I wrote you something on the back canvas, under the flap. Did you ever read it?"

"No." She never knew it was there.

"I hope you still have it." And he walked away.

"Of course I still had it but I wasn't letting on. I started looking for it as soon as I got home, ripping open old boxes and rummaging through some of the closets," Gram told me.

It turned up in a box she had from her dancing days, along with performance programs and some sketches from Joe.

"My past." She smirked.

"And?" I asked, enraptured.

She took a sip of her tea and cleared her throat. "The painting was of a bouquet of flowers. I peeled back the flap and there was the loveliest letter he had ever written. It was, I suppose, a goodbye letter."

That was all she said and that said it all.

When Joe returned to Gram's life there was no bitterness from the past. She had let the past go a long time ago and was enjoying the attention he bestowed upon her even if it was through the local mailman.

A year to the day after Joe found Gram, he sent her an anniversary card and wrote, "Whether you consider this our first or fifty-eighth year, this, the beginning of an additional one. We turn another page of our book in grateful compliant anticipation of what the future holds. There is harmony and consistency in all God's works. Happy Anniversary Vivian. As Ever, Joe."

Once they reconnected, they never let go. They helped each other through the aging process, lamenting and joking about their bodily afflictions. They sent each other gifts through the mail and spoke and wrote to each other every few days for the next fifteen years.

When Gram was ninety-four, Joe's kidneys failed and he had to go for dialysis. She agonized over it because her friend Angie, in the nursing home, had the same thing happen and she eventually passed away from it. Now, Gram was trying to make peace with the love of her life dying a slow and painful death too, the same way her brother Percy died.

She and Joe exchanged letters that went from sweet and lovely to depressing and sad with age. They were both forlorn about their aging bodies and persisting medical conditions.

"I still feel young but my body is giving out," she often told me. It would make me terribly sad when she spoke like that because I knew it was true.

When I was around eight and she would refer to getting old, I would say, "Don't worry Gram. By the time that happens, it will be the future. I will be rich and can buy you all new body parts so you can live forever." I believed it then. Now, I wished it were true.

After a year on dialysis, Joe transferred into a nursing facility as well. Now they were both in homes for the aged and it was a one-way ticket in.

Joe wrote less and less during that year but they continued to talk on the phone. In his last birthday card to her, he wrote, "I want to assure you; that chamber in my heart is still occupied by the memory of you. Let us remember: memories now, more than ever, are like roses in our December."

When Gram was ninety-six the letters stopped. "I haven't heard from Joe in a few weeks." She shot me a casual glance as she fiddled with her pizza but I saw right through it.

Our pizza lunch turned serious. "What can I do Gram?"

"Nothing Totie, I'm just glad you are here today."

His daughter called Gram a few days later. He passed away peacefully.

I went to see her right away. Many times my grandma hid her sadness from me. She thrived on being strong and independent. I wasn't sure how she'd react this time.

She was in her wheelchair watching *Jeopardy* and having a jelly donut. Gram was always dressed up but today was more formal in a violet blouse with an antique ivory broach, charcoal dress pants, her face adorned with light blue eye shadow and pink lipstick. She was wearing her signature Charlie perfume and if anyone commented on that, she'd smirk her usual reply, "I have to be ready when I meet my maker."

But I knew the truth; inside she was hurting. There was no funeral to attend; she wouldn't go see Joe after all these years for the first time and for the last time. Instead she sat there dressed up, honoring and mourning the love of her life.

"I am so sorry Gram." I said and hugged her tight.

"I know you are Totie." She sighed, smiling through her grief. "It'll be time for me too. I can't live forever. I've watched my friends and siblings all go before me."

I hated that she was right. At ninety-six, she was sad she was the last one remaining. With the love of her life, Joe, gone along with her brothers Clifford, Percy and Buddy, I thought about psychic Susan's prediction. I told Gram about the supposed heaven welcoming committee right after the reading and she was quite amused saying, "I hope that's true. I would love to see my brother Percy again." Now she would add Joe to that list.

Despite Susan's reading being incorrect about Gram passing in four months, I always hoped that her last sentence were true, "she will be greeted in heaven by her brothers and the love of her life." What more could we wish for in our soul's journey? To make that transition with the people we love waiting on the other side for us with open arms.

Gram taught me a master class in life. I hoped a reward of such magnitude was on the other side for her. But I didn't know at the time if the prediction was accurate.

Years later, I would eventually find out that there was some truth in Susan's prediction and Gram would get her wish.

A Prayer with Whipped Cream on Top

Ten years after Joe and Gram revived their romance, my mom found her on the floor of her apartment in a pool of blood. The muscle in her throat was tightening and bleeding internally for a while. She never alerted us about the difficulty she was having swallowing her food. She began choking, sending her into a coughing spasm and then rupture. She was barely conscious and rushed to the ER for throat surgery.

We sat through the surgery and she pulled through. The nurse came out and said we could go in for a visit. I expected her to be groggy, not unconscious. The only sound in her room that day was hissing machines and intermittent beeps. Her neck was wrapped in a big bandage and medical tape, looking as if she were wearing a giant white scarf. Without her wig, her thin white hair advanced her age. For the first time, I saw Gram as old and fragile.

The staff suggested we leave and come back the next day. We kept calling that night and still the same. Still unconscious.

"Time will only tell," they told us.

This was the first time Gram had ever been in a hospital aside from giving birth. And now her first time was life threatening. That night, after I left the hospital, I went home, worrying the whole way. Would this be it? Would Gram make it? I said little prayers throughout the day for her recovery but pedestrian prayers weren't good enough. I needed the express lane to the Universe, a prayer with whipped cream on top.

I remembered what Laura, a co-worker, told me a few months before. We were on lunch break at a sales meeting and we were talking about faith and spirituality. She was having trouble in her relationship and needed to move out but couldn't find a place. "I found a quiet spot, lit a candle and asked for what I needed." Two days later she signed the lease to her new apartment.

I was impressed and intrigued. This was the first time I had actually heard about this sort of prayer. I grew up reciting "Now I lay me down to sleep" prayers and prayed to God a few times a week asking for health and happiness for myself and of those I loved but had never heard it explained quite that way. It was more intentional, less habitual, more spiritual, less religious. Somewhat meditational and that appealed to me.

I dug around for a candle and found a pretty lavender pillar I was saving for a special occasion. I figured this was as special as it's ever going to get. I never prayed in front of a lit candle before but I was willing to try whatever it took. I lit the candle on my dresser and knelt down in front of it on the rug, imagining God seeing my flickering candle in the dark universe.

God? It's me, Kristin. I have a favor to ask even though I know you are very busy. But I need this. Please bless Gram and have her recover. I need her to stay and not leave me yet. We have a special bond and I want her in my life. She's not ready to go yet. She wants to be here too. I hope that you will please answer my prayer because I love her so much. Amen.

Mystical thirteenth century poet Rumi said, "If you can't pray sincerely, offer your dry, hypocritical prayer, for God in his mercy accepts bad coin."

I was going for sincere.

I prayed with all my might and felt connected and tapped into something bigger. I think it was an early appearance in my life of what I now think of as the power of intention. I had been doing that prior by just being positive in life but not in a conscious or meditational sort of way. It was out of my control and her life was in God's hands. All I could do was ask. Besides, isn't it the believing behind the asking that makes it work?

The next morning I arranged to meet my mom at 9 a.m. in Gram's hospital room. The churning in my stomach wouldn't stop. I feared seeing what I saw the night before; a frail lady without her wig and makeup, silent and sleeping, slipping away from me. I feared my prayer hadn't worked.

I wouldn't let fear rob me of my spiritual connection from last night. I rode the elevator alone, closed my eyes and for good measure whispered a pleading reminder to the heavens, "Please God."

Walking down the stark white hallway passing several rooms on the way, I folded my arms across my chest; unsure if it was the actual temperature or the chill I get when I'm nervous. The rooms were filled with people just like Gram; sick and not knowing the outcome of their situation. They were probably praying, just like me, for convalescence. I took a deep breath and walked into her room.

"Hi Totie!" There she was, sitting up in bed, applying coral lipstick with a round hand held mirror.

I couldn't believe my eyes. The same eyes that focused on the flickering candle were now staring at Gram, the dainty little lady in her floral pink nightie.

I loved that candle.

Her recovery was bittersweet because she never went home after that, transferring instead into a nursing facility. Between an ongoing battle with rheumatoid arthritis and her new throat condition, my mom was concerned about Gram living alone. Gram struggled with the lack of privacy and independence she felt living in the facility.

It took some time but she became a star in the nursing home, or God's Waiting Room, as she called it. When she got sad about living there I tried to cheer her up, "There must be a reason for you to still be here Gram. You still have work to do."

My spiritual belief is that you are here to work out your soul's flaws and contribute your specialness to the world. Gram was still doing that, living with purpose.

When she was depressed after she first arrived, the head nurse had a psychologist come for a visit. Gram wound up giving her advice on her relationship.

I was like a celebrity because I was Vivian's granddaughter. "Oh my God! We love her!" the staff shrieked. All the nurses and administrative staff would bring her goodies, pick up things she needed at the store and go in for chats on their breaks just to sit with her. On First Annual Awards Night, she was given the "Most Spiritual" award. It was a mock gold toned Oscar, which she proudly displayed on her TV set.

Her room was decorated with gifts from adoring friends and people she'd met along the way. She had drawers full of chocolates, flowers in vases, and stacks of greeting cards and notes. The mail lady said, "Vivian keeps me busy. I'm always here with a package or card from someone. She is one popular lady."

Life is energy and what you put forth is what you get back. She gave out love, truly listened to others and was fully present. People never forgot her; Joe was the finest example of that. She was a rose in his December.

Wine and Wafers

"I'm sorry Totie, you can't try the wine yet. Sit here, Gram will be right back," Gram said to me, exiting our row toward the flower filled altar. I was the only kid over ten not making communion in church that day.

Gram was an active member in St. Ann's Episcopal Church from the day she moved to Sayville, Long Island, circa 1960, after the death of second husband, Larry. She attended service every Sunday and also volunteered Tuesdays and Thursdays at the church's thrift shop. That's where she met her friend Doris twenty-five years ago, sorting through a sock donation from a department store. She brought me a pair home; the socks still had store tags on them, "Brand new, can you believe it Totie? And we're selling them for twenty-five cents!"

Doris is about five feet tall with short red hair and big blue eyes. I remember meeting her as a little girl but really getting to know her during the few years Gram was living in the nursing home. Doris came every week with baked treats prepared to talk politics, world affairs and God. She and Gram shared the uncommon blended opinion of how inspirational yet faulty organized religion can be.

St. Ann's was built in 1888. A stone church with Tiffany designed stained glass windows, it looks like it belongs in the Department 56 Dickens Village collection. I attended service with Gram because my parents didn't attend church. Still communion-less by fifth grade, Gram arranged private instruction so that I could be "official" and eat the wafers and drink the wine on Sundays.

I took religion classes in a lady's home for several weeks with two other kids until all the lessons were covered. There was no official ceremony; I never wore a miniature white wedding dress on communion day like all my Catholic friends.

I nudged Gram that Sunday because I wanted to finally try the garnet colored wine that matched my birthstone and that delicious wafer like all the other kids my age had already done. Finally came the announcement.

"Will our three special guests making first time communion today please approach the altar," Father said.

Gram grabbed my hand as we stood and walked up with the others. Kneeling down with Gram behind me, I folded my hands and the pastor placed the wafer in it. I left it there for him to dip it in the wine. Gram told me not to sip out of the cup because of germs. I took my first sip which created a glue-like reaction with the wafer, adhering to the roof of my mouth. It dissolved in my mouth while we walked back to our seats and sat. It wasn't as tasty as I had expected, what was the big deal? I looked over at Gram who was beaming at me. I laughed and snuggled into her arm, Gram winked and squeezed my hand. I squeezed back.

It never really bothered me one way or another that I hadn't made communion, I just liked going to church with Gram. It was our time together on Sundays when I had her all to myself. I never felt like I was missing out when I sat in the pew and waited for her return. But now knowing that it made Gram so happy and proud, I ate that up.

As an adult I feel that I don't need church to live a spiritual life. Even though I was baptized and made my communion, I never felt connected to church. The routine of it is something I don't enjoy. Sit up, sit down, make peace, take communion, make a donation, Amen. Same time next week. That's what it feels like to me.

God is everyday and everywhere; compassion to hurting friends, faith in struggles, banning together after 9-11, saving a drowning bee in the pool, appreciating the body as a masterpiece, the beauty and recognition of synchronicity. God is big but God is little too. God is in the noise and also in the silence. God's not just Sunday at 11 a.m.

I don't condemn churchgoers, I admire the commitment they have each week. But I knew early on that I would seek God in other places. My favorite of all is in nature. Standing by a waterfall, looking at the moon, snorkeling in the ocean, hiking in the woods, that is where I feel most connected to something bigger and deeper.

Initially though, I had fun while attending church with Gram that whole summer. I got to sleep over her house in the pull out couch all by myself. But then I got some devastating news at the start of sixth grade. With my brother John in college, my parents decided the three of us would move to Dunedin, Florida in October, leaving Gram behind. Mom and dad were making another go of their marriage.

I was heartbroken after moving and spent the next three months writing her I miss you letters while trying to make friends at my new school in the sunshine state.

Gram came to visit during Christmas and stayed for two weeks. I showed her around the neighborhood, the school I rode my bike to, the mall with the indoor ice-skating rink, the cookie place that made chocolate chip cookies the size of New York pizza and The Rocking Chair Movie Theater. I took her to see *E.T.* there with my mom, dad and John, who came home during college break. We all ate bright yellow popcorn and rocked back and forth in our seats while E.T. ate Reese's Pieces with his glowing finger.

I showed her everything she was missing.

She gave me money to buy more video games for my new Atari game system. My favorites were *Ms. Pac Man, Kaboom!, Donkey Kong* and *Frogger*. I was obsessed with *Frogger* and always held the highest score. I cracked up when the frog got hit by a car, while zigzagging across the highway and then splat into a big X. Now that's what I call a high tech 1980's video game.

It was that sunny Christmas in Florida where Gram came face to face with Pop-Pop aka Ben, her ex. I wondered how it would be being in the same house at the same time with my divorced grandparents. I had never seen them together before. Pop-Pop lived thirty minutes away from our new house. After the front door squeaked open, I heard Pop-Pops voice, "sure, sure" so I came bopping in the living room to give him a hug.

Gram stood behind me and said, "Hello, Benny," and gave a counterfeit smile.

"Hello there, Viv," said Pop-Pop, impeccably dressed in a pastel blue polo shirt and dress pants with shiny black shoes.

After the initial greeting they stayed on opposite sides of the house. Pop-Pop shared car-talk with Dad and John while me, mom and Gram went to the vacant lot next door and picked oranges off the trees. It was a new development so all the unsold lots were chock full of free oranges game for juicing. Later we went to the back yard, checked for gators (we were suspicious of the reservoir in back) and took a family photo as we sat at the picnic table. I sat between my two grandparents on the long redwood bench, one arm on each shoulder smiling a toothless grin while my brother stood and held our orange tabby cat, Freddy the Freeloader, upside down in his arms. My mom and dad stood behind us, smiling awkwardly. It's the only photo my mom has of her parents together since she was one.

The two weeks with Gram whizzed by. I made the most of every day with her, waking at eight for freshly squeezed orange juice and buttered english muffins, up past ten on *Dynasty* nights, gasping at the latest antics of Alexis Carrington.

I was never conscious of the day or time until one day Gram said, "Totie, I'm leaving Sunday."

Gram stayed until just after my birthday, January fifth. I put up a brave front at the airport but was crushed inside. I couldn't imagine living my whole life in Florida, away from my old neighborhood, my best friends and away from Gram.

Gram's love was like a homemade pie; sweet, warm, comforting and filling me in a way that only a dessert will do. When she wasn't around I was contest apple pie with a piece mysteriously gone. Only winning when she was there completing me.

I didn't stay sorrowful for long because by March, my mom packed it up and we moved back to Long Island, sans Dad. She hated living there and missed her friends and Gram. And unsolved martial problems don't disappear in a new geographic location; it just added more problems. It was the third or fourth reconciliation/split of my parents since their divorce, depending on your optimistic/pessimistic view.

I went back to the same sixth grade class but lived in a different neighborhood. I was happy to be back and having Gram only a few miles away. We had sleepovers on weekends for months where she made me homemade hot chocolate and a Thomas' english muffin with sliced banana for breakfast. To a six-grader that was gourmet stuff.

On Sundays, we went back to St. Ann's for wine and wafers.

Mexican Foam

"Totie, I'm so happy you broke the cycle of unsuccessful marriages in this family. Your mom, my mom and I never had any luck with men," Gram told me one Friday over mushroom pizza.

Gram was crazy about my husband Joe or "Chico," his initial nickname.

In 1996, I planned a girls' vacation week in Cancun with three friends, Angela, Lisa and Gina. Gina's boyfriend was going to meet us there, joining us the last four days of the trip. Two weeks prior to departure, he and Gina called it quits. We asked everyone we knew to take the fifth ticket, which he was giving away. There were no takers.

Five days before we were leaving, our friend Kevin asked his friend Joe, "Hey do you wanna go to Cancun with four girls?"

"Um, does the sun rise and set each day?" Joe responded and the fifth ticket was booked.

In Cancun we partied up a storm, hitting all the clubs and drinking one too many tequila poppers. Before going out one night we realized Joe arrived earlier that day. We called his room but he was out so we left a note under his door, MEET US AT THE FOAM PARTY AT CLUB OASIS.

We arrived in the club just as they started squirting foam onto the dance floor. The giant cannon was atop a stage squirting out frothy white suds high into the air where it plopped on the dance floor. It was the first time I had been to a foam party and we were all ready to dive right in. Lisa screamed over the music, "Let's go!" and off we went into the white abyss. As the foam was filling the dance floor, we danced the Macarena, trying not to slip and break any bones. The floor was getting slippery and the foam was now up to my waist. I had denim shorts on and my legs were wet and slimy as I sang "Hey Macarena, ayyy!"

"Do you remember what Joe looks like?" I asked Lisa in between song verses and dance moves. Lisa met Joe once at a party but the rest of us had never before met this guy from Queens.

"Yeah, I think he's got brown hair and light eyes." She answered.

I looked around at hundreds of bopping heads, "Yeah, um, he shouldn't be too hard to spot in this crowd," I joked.

An hour later, the foam rose up to our chest and tequila was being poured into our mouths from hospitable Mexican waiters.

"Weeee!" I gathered the foam into my hands and threw piles of it into the air, watching it float down onto my friends' heads.

"I'm soaked," I screamed over the music, "I don't think this guy is coming. We'll catch him tomorrow."

"Yeah, let's go in deeper, there's an open spot over there in the center," Angela yelled and pointed. And off we went into a cloud of bubbles.

Around 3 a.m., we arrived back at our hotel room, soggy and drunk. Someone had the bright idea of phoning Joe. Lisa dialed the phone, "Hi Joe? It's Lisa and the girls from the Cancun trip. What are you doing?" she giggled and held her hand over the mouthpiece, "I think he was sleeping." She continued, "Come down and say hi, we're in room 302," she paused. "Ok, see you in a few."

Five minutes later there was a knock on the door. Lisa swung open the door and we all screamed, "Hola Chico!"

"Hola Chicas!" Joe sung out in a thick Queens accent, holding a six-pack of Coronas. He glided into the room and shook all our hands, repeating each one of our names.

"Sorry I couldn't make the foam pahty, I went scuba divin' today and was wiped out. Let's hang out tomorra. We'll rent mopeds, hit the beach and then go fa cocktails," he said.

The four of us eagerly nodded our heads at the charming Sagittarian.

The next three days the five of us scootered around Cancun on mopeds, took a helicopter ride and partied like rock stars at Señor Frogs and LaBoom, two nightclubs known for rockstar status partying.

We had the best time altogether. I thought Joe was sweet and so much fun and we really became great friends on that trip. But I was in single mode, not looking for a relationship.

We boarded the plane on the last day and were snug in our seats when the flight attendant made an announcement, "Attention passengers, this flight is overbooked and we need volunteers to get off. You will be compensated and be given a flight home tomorrow." Joe and Lisa jumped up and said, "Let's do it."

Miss Goody Two Shoes, aka me, whined, "I can't, I have to work tomorrow." I had no vacation days left. Angela and Gina couldn't stay either.

Joe turned back half way down the aisle and asked, "Kristin, can you take my bag home? I already checked it. I'll call ya in the next few days so I can come and get it."

"No problem Chico. Have fun." I watched them run toward the cockpit.

Fate.

A few days later Joe called me to retrieve his bag. After reminiscing about Cancun, he invited all the chicas out to his summer rental in Hampton Bays. "We'll go to the beach and then go out fa cocktails."

"OK, I'll bring your bag and the photos from the trip. I have some incriminating ones of you," I teased.

The girls and I ventured out to Joe's house with his purple bag full of clothes. We went to the beach and afterward went to an outdoor beach bar. After an hour or two and a few beers, I took Joe's hand and pulled him on the dance floor. "Come on Chico, you owe me a dance for lugging your bag across the country."

"I owe ya big time. Come on Señorita." He twirled me around as I laughed. He was funny. I liked his playfulness.

We were dancing, reminiscing and laughing about our Mexican antics when we looked at each other and kissed.

He looked different in this light, close to home.

That was my last first kiss.

Everything and the Kitchen Sink

When I was four, I was in love with a thirty-five year old criminal named Sonny.

Sonny was a bi-sexual, gorgeous, Italian-American from New York who tried robbing a bank to pay for his boyfriend's sex change operation. If this sounds familiar, it's because it was the plot of the movie *Dog Day Afternoon* and Sonny the criminal was played by Al Pacino. It was love at first sight during the first movie I ever saw.

Despite the sexual content, violence, F bombs, the riot against the police and the eventual murder and capture of the robbers at the finale, it was one feel-good film for a child of four. My parents thought it was hysterical that I loved the movie and even more funny that I loved Al Pacino, who was thirty years my senior. So I found it strange to see the look of horror on other adults' faces when they asked what my favorite film was and I answered with a delightful, "*Dog Day Afternoon.*"

Despite a rough start in choosing love interests, I think I fared pretty well over the years. For the most part, my exes were nice guys but I never wanted to marry any of them. After the last breakup, I figured I'd cool it for a while and chill with my girlies. That's when we came up with the Cancun vacation. I frequently declared in those days, "I'm not looking for a boyfriend. I wanna be free for a while."

What's the phrase? Make a plan and God laughs?

∗∗∗

After my last first kiss, Joe and I became inseparable. We spent lazy days at the beach, bike riding, boating, and just being happy together. I was still in denial about how serious we were getting, figuring we met in Cancun, how serious can this get? Little by little, the other dates I was supposed to be having during my "single summer" were falling off the radar and I was spending my free time with Joe.

By the end of July and dating for two months, Joe mentioned that he had a big beach bash planned.

"Every few summers, I have a pahty on the beach to raise money for charity. There's a covah charge and the leftovah money goes to charity. I have a band, food, drinks and games. So don't make plans, you and the chicas have ta come."

"That sounds fun! Ooh, you should make it a pirate themed party and ask people to dress up," I urged.

Joe nodded, "yeah," while his eyes shimmered with zeal.

I continued on, "Ooohh and the chicas can dress as lady pirates with super soaker guns filled with tropical drinks and give shots to people on the beach!"

"Wow, that's a great idea. I'll buy the supplies," Joe said, grinning as he jotted notes in his palm pilot.

Ten days later, the chicas and I showed up in skimpy red, black and white striped pirate costumes with frayed mini skirts. The four of us walked toward the sand and found Joe policing the entrance, collecting money and giving out plastic bracelets for entry.

"It's the chicas! Hey, you girls look great. Here, I filled these up with Blue Hawaiians," he said, grinning as he handed us each a super soaker gun.

I slipped on my sparkly silver pirate eye patch.

"Oh Kristin, wait, before ya go off and get people polluted, come ovah here for a minute," leading me to the smoking six foot wide barbeque. Through the flames I looked to the other side and saw three women and a guy dripping with sweat, standing there flipping burgers and hot dogs.

"Kristin, this is my mom, brother, sister and aunt," Joe said as he pointed to them.

Joe's mom had a sweet round face, short blonde hair and a giant smile. Her eyes twinkled as she squealed, "Hi Sweetie, you look so cute."

They all looked up at me for the first time as they flipped burgers. Joe's siblings, Deirdre and Michael and his Aunt Ginger all waved hi with their greasy spatulas through the gray cloud of charcoal smoke and together greeted me differently in unison, "hi, what's up, hello dear."

"Uh, thanks. So nice to meet you," I said to his mom as I peered through the one eye that wasn't covered with a glittering eye patch, smoothing down my pirate skirt. I fidgeted with my soaker gun adjusting its strap, smiling and crumpling my toes in the sand as I waved back to his siblings and aunt.

"OK, we'll see ya later," Joe yelled over the building crowd. His family all giggled as we walked away.

I pumped my super soaker tank with potent turquoise liquid and walked off into the sandy crowd calling out, "Shots, blue Hawaiian shots!" while party guests opened their mouths wide.

✶✶✶

Joe and I still laugh about the Pirate Beach Party and my crazy first impression. The great thing was that his family never flinched. If anything, they thought of us as a great match.

My mother-in-law Joanie was a widow since Joe was eleven. She raised Joe and his two siblings in a one-bedroom apartment in Woodside, Queens. Joe and his brother shared a room while his mom and sister slept on a pullout couch in the living room. Joe was living solo in the same apartment when we met.

During the Summer of Joe, I was living at home with my mom and brother John, working in public relations and fund raising at a charitable organization. Gram had an apartment on the side of the house so I could see her whenever I wanted.

With Joe in Queens and me on Long Island, the commute between our homes was forty-five minutes so when we became serious we slept over each other houses two days a week to spend more time together.

Dating for five months, on the way back from fall apple picking, Joe asked, "What do ya think about movin' in togetha?"

He caught me off guard. I hadn't thought of it. "Like when?" I gulped.

"Soon," he said, laughing.

I went to college locally and never left home. What would my mom and Gram do without me? What would I do without them? Plus it was so quick. Didn't people date like five years before they shacked up? I was just getting used to the notion that Joe wasn't the summer fling I sucked face with in the Hamptons. He had substance; we had promise.

It wasn't a completely deluded proposition. I kinda liked the idea. "Maybe, let me think about it."

A few days later I was sitting in Gram's apartment eating grilled cheese sandwiches when I told my mom and Gram about Joe's suggestion. My mom finished chewing and said, "That's a big step. But I really like Joe and you are the perfect couple. Are you considering it?"

Gram waited for my mom to end her sentence then jumped in, "Totie, he can't buy the milk and not the cow! Will you eventually get married?"

"Yes Gram that is a possibility but we wanna try living together first. We're tired of all the driving back and forth and don't want to jump into a marriage right away. That will come in time. We love each other and want to be together."

Joe's invitation to shack up had grown on me the last few days and I was now liking the idea and was ready to defend it.

Gram was crazy about Joe so she seemed satisfied with my answer saying, "I guess that's what you kids do nowadays."

Later when Joe came over we were playing Dominos when I said, "Oh yeah, is that offer still good?" looking up from my pile of dominos.

He looked up to see me smirking, answering, "Why, yes, yes it is," throwing down a double domino, trying to stump me.

"Ok, let's do it!" I sang out. "But Gram wants to make sure that there's no free milk going on here. Eventually, you may have to buy the cow."

Amused, Joe, said, "Yes, I promise that will come in time. I will buy the cow."

"Mooo," I said as I placed my last domino on the end of the train to win the game, then I ran to the other side of the table to give him a victory kiss.

✷✷✷

By December, we found an apartment twenty minutes away and centrally located to both of our jobs. We were going to sign the lease when I stated, "Sprinkles is moving in too."

"What?" We hadn't discussed my cat coming to live with us. Joe had never owned a cat before.

"That's the deal Joe; if you want me, my cat comes too. It's non-negotiable." I meant it.

"OK, Mr. Sprinkles too." Joe replied.

I adopted Sprinkles before I met Joe. I was working at an ad agency and someone in the office had kittens for adoption. By the time she got to me, she only had one left, the runt of the litter. I agreed sight unseen.

She brought him to me the next day in a ladies shoebox. I looked down and sitting on a washcloth was a tiny kitten with shiny licorice fur and brown highlights. I put the box in my lap, petted his soft fuzzy back and said, "Hi little boy. I'm your new mommy."

He looked up at me with little round aquamarine eyes that blinked as he purred and sniffed my hand. Then he jumped out of the box crawled up my chest and sat on my shoulder nuzzling my hair. At just seven weeks old, he knew then that I was his mom and always would be.

He had a larger than life personality and I swear he understood every word I was saying. When my dad stayed with us he chuckled with amusement, "That cat knew you were coming home. He jumped up in the window just before you pulled up in the driveway." We were connected.

He had a funny way of shaking his tail when he was excited. When I opened the fridge, his tail stood up straight while it quivered rapidly. Then he let out a very distinct and demanding meow that translated into, "I'm hungry again." He made me laugh every day.

Sprinkles was aloof with Joe, the new man in my life, even after being bribed with treats. Sprinkles saw right through it but ate them anyway. Whenever we were sitting together, Sprinkles came and plopped down on my lap facing his backside to Joe, which meant in cat sign language, "You stole my mommy."

I hoped this living arrangement would work out.

One month later I moved all my belongings into my new apartment with Joe. On my last trip I got out the cat carrier and placed Sprinkles in it on his favorite blue blanket. Gram came over from her apartment next door to say goodbye to me with mom and John. My brother gave me a kiss and wished me luck. Gram held my hands tightly and said, "You're all grown up now. But you'll always be my little Totie. I'll see you soon darling. Be happy always."

My mom hugged me with tears in her eyes and said, "I know you and Joe will be very happy together. I'm not losing you, I'm winning Joe."

"I love you very much. Talk to you tomorrow, " I said as my voice quivered. I'll see them tomorrow during unpacking so there is nothing to cry about, I thought.

I placed Sprinkles in the car, fastened my seat belt, drove down the street and burst into tears. As I passed my neighbor's houses on the street and rounded the corner I yelled at myself, "Why are you crying? This is supposed to be fun and happy!" Then I answered myself, "I don't know why I'm crying. It's stupid. I'm moving a half hour away."

I looked down at Sprinkles, who was staring at me. I wiped my tears and stuck my finger through the cage's opening to scratch his furry cheek.

"Don't worry babycat, you'll be OK. You'll like your new home. Mommy will take care of you," I whimpered.

He nuzzled my finger with his nose and mouth and licked it. I looked through the window of the carrier again and he was staring at me calmly. His paws were folded underneath his chest showing contentment. He was happy to be with me, it didn't matter where that was. I thought I was consoling him but he was consoling me.

My tears were dried and my eyes were clear now, I pressed the accelerator, moving faster on the road ahead.

Within one week Joe built Sprinkles a new perch on the front window by the door of our two-bedroom apartment. The yard was full of trees, singing birds and flying insects - reality TV for cats. We all liked the new place and were fixing it up and making it our own with photos, new curtains and furniture we picked out together. The move was seamless and we got along from the start aside from the solitary closet we both wanted to stuff with our own things.

The first few days Sprinkles was sniffing around Joe's things and giving him the stink eye. He let Joe pet him once or twice before scooting away. A week later Joe came home with salmon flavored cat treats that drove Sprinkles crazy. Every chance he got, Joe jiggled the bag then waved one in the air. Sprinkles cautiously approached until Joe dropped the treat to the floor. Sprinkles darted over, vacuumed it up and ran away. It took half a bag or so but Sprinkles accepted this new man in our life and eventually bossed Joe around the kitchen, signaling to him when it was snack or meal time. And salmon cat treats were always on the shopping list.

One day I came home from work and Sprinkles was waiting at the door. He looked lonely. At my mom's house there had been three people plus another cat for company. In his new pad, he was by himself all day. He needed a sibling. Hmm, how would I broach this subject with Joe? I'll wait a few weeks since he is getting used to one cat right now.

Lilly Francis McNuggets appeared at exactly the right time a few weeks later.

We were at a birthday party in the Richmond Hill section of Queens for one of Joe's relatives. We skipped dessert to go to this legendary, old fashioned ice-cream parlor, Jahn's. It served an ice-cream sundae called The Kitchen Sink. Need I say more?

After our thirty-two scoop Kitchen Sink started to turn into a big soupy mess, we left Jahn's and walked around. A few doors down was a pet shop. "Let's go in," I suggested, testing Joe's openness for a new pet.

The relationship was new so of course the answer was, "OK honey."

Someone in the neighborhood dropped off a litter of seven-week old kittens. They were all curled up in their cage. When we approached the cage, the little brown tiger striped kitten with the white bib came right over and stood on her back legs and let out a squeaky meow. The shop owner took her out and the kitten snuggled me as her little motor purred. I took her interest as a sign and decided she would make a perfect addition to our little family.

"Joe, isn't she cute?" I said, batting my eyes and waving her tiny paw at him.

"Very," he patted her head and stroked her cheek.

"Sprinkles is lonely and needs a friend. I want to adopt this kitten," I said as I held her up cheek to cheek staring at Joe.

Five minutes later, we were at the counter with Lilly in a new carrier and a case of kitten food. I plead a mean case.

Sprinkles embraced Lilly, teaching her to swat, play with mousies and run around the apartment. He also kissed her head and cuddled with her in one big ball. Sprinkles was Lilly's hero. She followed him around, imitating his jumps and learning his bird watching skills and first hand how to swarm a fridge.

Lilly was a mama's girl who was well behaved, had a fear of being picked up and liked to hold my hand with her paw. Lilly's eyes looked like faceted emerald gemstones. Looking into them, I saw depth and understanding. I think she was an old soul.

Like any good pet parents, Sprinkles and Lilly became one of the most important aspects of our life together. We became a little family, part fur, part skin.

Mom and Gram both loved Joe from the start and recognized our compatibility. We both love *The Sound of Music*, chocolate egg creams, packing a suitcase, a warm beach, reggae music, organic food, skiing, Italy, sipping rum punch in the Caribbean, our cats, Broadway shows, swimming, conspiracy theories, unpacking a suitcase at home, family, and life. Joe loves life as much as me. We would both do almost anything on a whim.

Together in our little apartment, I sat with Joe next to me, Lilly on my lap and Sprinkles on the arm of the couch next to me. We were watching *Dog Day Afternoon*. "Joe, this was my favorite movie when I was four. I had a crush on Sonny."

"Really?" he laughed.

I hugged him tight and petted the cats as Sonny entered the getaway car ready to start his new life. I held my breath remembering the ending.

Grateful life was good in that moment. I have it all, I thought. Everything and the kitchen sink.

Sparkling Joy

"I knew he was the one," my mom said looking up, licking the ninety-ninth wedding invitation.

During our first "official" date, Joe showed up with a picnic basket and pink champagne and we rode our bikes to the park. As we were riding along Main Street, I heard a honk and there's my mom, passing by in her Honda Accord, waving.

"I knew it when I saw you guys riding bikes on your first date," she boasted, placing the "love" stamp on the envelope.

She also picked Joe out of the Cancun video I was showing everyone.

"Who's that?" she asked, pointing to Joe on the TV screen. "He's cute."

My mom's been known to be psychic on occasion, having little premonitions here and there, even dreaming the death of the Queen Mother the night before she passed. Call it ESP or simply mother's intuition.

Gram asked me questions when I got back from Mexico. She wanted to hear all the details of who went, what we did and what the heck was Chichen Itza?

I loved coming home and sharing my adventures and photos with her. But I didn't slip Joe into the conversation until a few weeks later when we were going on our first bicycle date. Joe charmed the pants off of my family starting with champagne mimosas in a wicker basket strapped to handlebars.

Sprinkles was the only hold out. When Joe came over, he disappeared into the cellar saying to himself in cat language, "This bozo won't even make it past summer then I'll be back in the drivers seat. Meow."

So you can see why Sprinkles nurturing me in the car heading to our new apartment was a bigger moment than a fearful girl with her finicky feline. It was really, one small step for girl, one giant leap for cat.

After Joe's immersion into Cat Kingdom, we played for keeps. We both hinted around the possibility of marriage so I guessed it was coming sooner or later.

We got engaged six months after the shack up and married a year after that. I had both of my parents walk me down the aisle and I had a special limo take Gram and her friend home. At eighty-seven, it was the first time Gram ever rode in a limo.

We joked about having Sprinkles and Lilly come to the wedding like people who have their dogs as their ring bearers.

We interviewed three wedding officials of varying denominations. It was Toby we liked. He was a United Methodist Minister we found through a friend. He was funny, warm, smart and understood we wanted to be married outside by the water by someone who was flexible in their ideology about God.

We met with Toby in his house for several weeks before the wedding and filled him in on the plans, the excitement and our future goals. We discussed love, God and commitment.

After our last meeting I had a revelation and said to Joe, "You know what the saddest part of marriage is? If we are married for like fifty years, we'll lose all our loved ones then eventually each other. One of us will witness the death of the other."

"Hopefully that's a long time away hon and something we can't control," Joe assured me.

"I know but I still think it's sad. I want us all to be together forever."

"What makes you think that we won't? You can believe anything you want to believe. I tell myself I will see my dad again someday," he said.

Joe was my grief opposite. His grief began so young and his inventory grew through the years. I was lucky to not know the actual heartache of grief. I had only my fear.

As we faced each other on our wedding day, Toby stood before us under blue skies. He looked out at our family and friends and said, "When I was a kid, there were no rail road crossings so we had to pay attention as we crossed the railroad tracks. As I stand before you now, I want to offer Joe and Kristin the same advice. Stop. Look. And Listen."

Toby turned to us and continued, "Stop," he paused and smiled. "Stop planning and controlling. Enjoy your wedding day, even the things that aren't perfect. Slow down, don't miss the moments. Look. Look around at all the people here that love you and support this union. Listen. Listen to what people say, especially those you love. The words are only spoken once."

Later, when they rolled our devils food and raspberry cake with white chocolate fondant icing out I turned to Joe and said, "Look around. Let's always remember this moment."

Before slicing, I looked around at everyone. The lights were dimmed and we lit sparklers so the tent was exploding with bursts of light everywhere. Our family and friends waved their sparklers around while their luminous faces exuded joy. The *Peanuts* theme song played while Joe and I held hands. Our other hands held sparklers connecting our light to everyone else's in the glitter filled tent. I was forever grateful in that moment. It was mine to keep forever. All the people I loved were under that tent.

Better than the cake, I could taste the joy. It had a flavor. Simple and sweet.

Sprinkles

I could not get out of bed to face the day. Five more minutes, five more hours, maybe if I laid there longer it would all go away. My eyes stung and the corners stuck together with dried salt. I listened to the quietness of my house. It wasn't quiet serenity. It was dead silence.

I forced myself out of bed and walked into the spare bedroom where he died. The door squeaked open. Everything was as it should be: made bed, photo of Venice hanging on the wall, candle on the dresser. No sign of anything unusual until I looked down. There on the floor was his little body laying motionless on a blanket in our rectangular laundry basket. Joe must have done that early this morning.

I walked into the bathroom where we tried multiple breathing treatments. I stood in the doorway of our makeshift medical room and looked around, there was no evidence of the distress of the past few days. Fearing a reminder, Joe sanitized the room and swiped it all away leaving no trace of sickness and despair. No syringes, no medicine, no IV, the beige tile and vanity were gleaming with a faint smell of vinegar cleaning solution.

I looked around for the claw. Joe mistakenly threw that away too. I found it on the bathroom floor the day before and placed it on the toilet tank thinking it would be a little genetic piece of my cat in case he didn't make it. From my thoughts to God's ears, Sprinkles, my beloved black cat, was dead.

While I moped around the house, in intermittent tears, the man of the house marshaled his sadness in a fashion straight out of a *Home*

Improvement episode. He left and returned from Home Depot with lots of wood. Joe was going to build the mother of all cat coffins.

Sprinkles deserved it and Joe needed an outlet for his grief. He spent hours that Tuesday in our backyard measuring, cutting, sawing and nailing while I spent part of the day upstairs petting my dead cat in his laundry basket gurney. I could hear the power saw outside as Joe made the cuts of wood. The sounds were vibrating my chest, jostling my heart.

I petted him, kissed him and talked to him. I wasn't even sure if this was sane or sanitary but I didn't care. I tried to find peace in the act. When I told my mom I was doing this she called and spoke to a vet tech at the animal hospital who said medically there was no harm in not burying the cat for a few days. "Nothing will happen to the body in that short amount of time," she assured. And spiritually she thought it was an excellent idea to find closure, much like humans do at a wake or funeral. I was told, "It helps to see the body."

At the end of the day, Joe came inside and yelled out, "I'm finished." He was pale, sweaty and his hazel eyes were despondent. In his arms was a square pine cat casket with silver hinges so the door could open and close. He hugged me as we stood in front of it and he said, "I think you should make it pretty." I agreed.

He pulled away and stammered, "We need to pick a spot, a spot fa the grave, fa the burial."

I couldn't decide if I wanted it out of sight so I wouldn't be reminded of his death all the time or if I wanted it in full view so I could remember his life whenever I looked outside. I decided on the latter. And so across the yard from our kitchen's sliding glass door, Sprinkles would be laid to rest forever, under an old black walnut tree.

The next morning I worked on the coffin at my kitchen table. Normally I liked the smell of freshly cut wood but as the box lay in front of me I breathed through my mouth fearing I'd hate that smell forever. Pulling out my craft box I decided to paint the coffin sky blue. I liked that color. It was peaceful and heavenly. I dipped the brush in and out of the paint cup. Back and forth my brush covered the wood with blue until the whole box glistened. When the initial coat was dried, I chose a midnight blue and painted:

Rest in Peace.

Sprinkles Lavin.

1994 – 2007

I always loved drawing cat faces so I added one. A black circle with three triangles: two on top for ears and one upside-down in the center of the circle for the nose. I painted that one pink. I added two almond shaped eyes and filled them in with aqua blue paint. The final touch… long gray whiskers.

It looked juvenile, like something I would have done in seventh grade art class. My seventh-grader portrait in honor of him.

I put my paintbrush down and looked outside through the glass door. Joe was digging a giant hole. It was done with the greatest of care and with the highest of purpose. With each shovel full of dirt thrown back my heart sank deeper into that hole. I stared at the man I married. How can my heart be so filled with pain and love at the same time?

It was December and already cool so our cat was resting in the coffin-laundry basket on the outside balcony of our house. His own little chilly funeral parlor where we could visit with him until his plot was ready and we could say our final goodbye.

The paint was dry and the coffin was done. Joe gently placed him inside on a soft pinstriped blanket with all his favorite things; a photo of us, a purple bouncy-ball, a play-mouse. We included these things so he wouldn't be scared. It would be dark when we closed the lid.

"Hon, you should put a lock of your hair inside." Joe grabbed the kitchen shears from the drawer and snipped off a half inch of my wavy brown hair and placed it inside next to his fuzzy belly.

I brought his cold, furry body in the house several times in those three days to mourn and make my peace. I had tremendous guilt whether or not I had made the right decisions with his veterinary care and feared I didn't do enough.

The guilt and sadness were eating away at me. I felt solely responsible for his demise.

Joe had organized a big family reunion down in Turks and Caicos and a few days before we were leaving, Sprinkles became sick and was not eating. The trip was paid for and twenty of Joe's relatives were flying down. I could not leave our sick cat. Joe, the eternal optimist, thought I was being paranoid and he would be fine. But I knew something wasn't right.

"No, he's never not eaten and been this lethargic," I pleaded. He wasn't even eating his treats anymore. We decided Joe would go and I would stay back. If he recovered I would meet Joe down there. That never happened.

I took Sprinkles to the vet who said he wasn't eating because his liver was failing. "Sometimes they pull through and sometimes they don't," the vet said.

It was my worst nightmare coming to fruition. Sprinkles' death was not an option. I would do everything possible, including begging for mercy. Later I prayed, God, please help me to cure my cat. Please don't take him from me. I love him so much. Please make him better. Amen.

I prayed a version of that same prayer over and over again.

I know from my job in the vitamin industry that the liver can regenerate so I began trying to make him healthy from the ground up. I would rebuild his strength and heal him. The vet had given me some liver medicine and I researched some additional things I could do.

A co-worker said she cured her cat from liver disease by force-feeding her cat through syringes. I tried that. For days before and after Joe left on the trip, I was chasing Sprinkles around and squirting high calorie food into his mouth. It takes a lot of syringes full of cat food to make a meal so it was basically a twenty-hour gig.

I slept a few hours and the next day I started over again with milk thistle, garlic, NAC, water and syringes full of mushy stinky cat food, which wound up on walls, furniture and me. If I was lucky I squirted most of it in his mouth. He would see me coming and run under the furniture or into a closet. The sight of me now equaled another pill or me shoving a syringe of food down his throat. He hated the taste of all the vitamins and because cats can't spit, he foamed at the mouth. My sick cat was afraid of me, it totally sucked.

I did this every twenty minutes for the next five days. If other cats got better, why couldn't he? He was totally healthy before this, running around the house playing and meowing.

I updated Joe daily by phone and my mom came over to help me out several times. But when I was alone, I felt really alone. I was petrified of him dying and to make it worse, dying when Joe was gone. I was tired and stressed but I did not give up. I thought that I would make him better. That's what I did. I made things better.

Even though he wasn't eating nearly the food he would normally eat, I saw that he was ingesting the food in the syringe along with the medicine and vitamins. A good sign.

Several days into it, he ate a handful of dry food and some of his all-time favorite, asparagus, on his own. I finally made a breakthrough, I thought. He's going to make it. My tenacity, hope and prayers worked. He purred as he ate and I petted him and smiled, feeling relieved and happy.

The next day, the sun was shining and as I got out of bed, I thought, he's on the road to recovery. I looked around the house and couldn't find him. After fifteen minutes of searching, I found him in the closet. I reached in and lifted him out when I heard him coughing and wheezing. This can't be, I thought. He ate yesterday. He wasn't coughing. He was doing better. Maybe he caught a cold. I rushed him back to the vet.

After hearing abnormalities in his chest, the vet sent me to coronary veterinary specialists at the Animal Emergency Clinic. After an ultra-sound the specialist said his heart was enlarged. "He has cardiomyopathy. I recommend heart medication and to stay for a day or two on oxygen. Then we'll see."

The specialist never made a promise for his recovery but never took away my hope. I felt like I was on the rollercoaster ride from hell. He's sick, he's better, he's worse. I was on the upside-down loop at that point and about to be sick.

I walked out the door with my empty pet carrier. I opened the door of my hybrid and placed the carrier inside, feeling defeated. Hoping I made the right decision, I slumped into my seat and put my head on the cold steering wheel. I felt relief and anxiety simultaneously. He was in the hands of professionals but I was petrified that he would die while he was there and while Joe was still away.

I went back later that night during visiting hours. I curled up on the floor beside his oxygen tank, which doubled as a cage. The staff took him out for a few minutes and he sat on my lap and purred. The female tech said, "Poor little guy. He is so sweet." Then she put him back in. I tried hard not to cry. I'm sure I looked pathetic to the staff. While they scurried around the animal hospital saving lives, I sat on the floor praying and talking through the glass to my boycat. His eyes were closed a lot but he sometimes looked at me through the glass with questioning eyes.

Before leaving, I left him one of Lilly's toys and a scarf of mine for scent plus a photo of me so he didn't think I deserted him. I went back the next day twice.

By the third day there, he was jaundiced due to major liver failure from not being force-fed anymore and his breathing was just a little better. He had a yellow tinge to his ears, skin and eyes, something I had never seen before.

In the exam room, Sprinkles sat on the table, weak and yellow. I soothed him by petting and talking to him. As I did that my mind was racing, what now, what now? They wanted to do more testing, more blood work, a scope down his throat to see if there was something else wrong.

Looking back, I knew what was wrong. He was dying and I wasn't letting him.

In those minutes to myself, I decided against it and would take him home. He wasn't improving there so I needed that last chance at home. The vet said I had to give him Sub Q fluids with a needle under his skin, give him two different types of heart medication plus I would have to try the force-feeding again. Tenacious but doubting my nursing skills, I looked to my mom who joined me in the exam room. "You can do it. I'll show you how," she said.

They sent me home with heart pills, medical syringes, I.V. fluids and hope. I paid the three thousand dollar vet bill and walked out with my cat thinking I'd start over again. They never asked me if I wanted the dreaded other option. And I didn't ask.

Joe came straight from the airport and met us at the Animal Emergency Clinic. We put Sprinkles in the car next to me in the back seat while Joe drove and my mom followed us. He purred the whole ride home. I was relieved Joe made it back from the trip and Sprinkles was alive. Now we would work as a team. We couldn't lose.

We arrived at the house and my mom immediately began giving me lessons on the IV fluids. Where to puncture the skin by his shoulders with the needle, how to hold the bag up high so the fluids would drip thru the clear plastic hose and flood his body under the skin which would eventually absorb into his body. After a few times of practice into a piece of fruit I had it down.

She knew how much Sprinkles meant to me and so he meant a lot to her. Next, she showed me how to give him injections. He needed a shot once a day. I had never given a shot to myself or anyone else so I sat attentively for another lesson. Fill the syringe with the medicine, hold it up, tap out the bubbles, pull back the plunger, pull up some loose skin on the cat and insert the sanitary metal point into him. Easy. I was becoming Kristin Lavin R.N.

Being Miss Vitamingirl, I was unfamiliar with all the meds and equipment that went along with serious disease but I learned quickly. Another living being was relying on me to live. I decided if I thought about that too much, I'd panic so I just focused on the here and now and the task I had to perform. I kept my faith so I could give Sprinkles one hundred percent of myself. Plus I always think like Scarlett O'Hara in times of stress, I'll think about that tomorrow. Tomorrow is another day. Cue musical soundtrack.

The next day he was the same and we agonized over the decision of putting him down. I was feeling anxious thinking about it especially if there was one slight chance of survival. Giving up hope was not in my genetic make-up. Looking at him I had a fleeting thought, is all this in his best interest or mine?

That evening I watched *Peaceful Warrior*, an indie film about a restless young gymnast who meets a spiritual guide who teaches him about life's meaning and purpose.

It's funny how information is given to you at the time you need it most. The movie's message was to live in the moment and be grateful for the present. After I watched it I thought how if my cat died now, I wasn't present with him, just loving him. I was in the future moment worrying what may happen or I was in the past, worried about decisions I had made. No wonder he was looking at me strangely, he was wondering where I had gone.

Later, I said a different type of prayer for my cat, please God, do not let him suffer. If you can't let him stay with us then take him peacefully at home. I don't want to have to make the decision to put him down. I love him so much and am grateful for every minute I have with him. Amen.

I surrendered. Whatever will be will be. No more vets, no more testing. He'll either get better or worse so I decided above all, I will be here now with him. He is alive now. This may be the end so I will cherish the life that is left.

The following day my mom came over to give moral support and lend some of her nursing skills so I could enjoy my time with him. She gave him the fluids and the shot while I petted and talked to him. My inner light had changed, lit by faith. Not the kind that he would get better but by the kind that no matter what happened he'd be OK and so would I.

By the afternoon, he perked up, walked around and jumped on the back of the chair. The past week, he hobbled around. My mom put her arm around my shoulder and looked at Sprinkles with a smile saying, "He looks like he may be getting better. Do you feel better?" She hated seeing me so sad.

"A little," I lied. Deep down I feared in my heart it was his last day and that spurt of energy was his last hoorah.

After his energetic display, Sprinkles laid down on the couch. I lay next to my cat while Joe drove my mom home. It was just us. No vets, no medicine, no distractions. Alone again.

I petted his un-groomed fur and kissed his head. It smelled like dried up cat food. He wasn't his usual clean self and I am sure that pissed him off. He took pride in self-grooming his silky coat and it never looked this bad. I stroked his fur with a damp washcloth to clean and console him. He purred his usual loud motor. I crouched down and sat, we were face-to-face, eye-to-eye.

"Whatever you decide, it's OK. I am so grateful to have you in my life and will love you forever," I said kissing him between his ears.

He stared back at me with such love. His eyes rolled back and closed. I panicked. Please not now. I got hysterical. I started crying and gasping for breath. "Please," I whimpered, "not right now baby." His eyes opened and grew really wide. He was still with his eyes upon me while I caught my breath.

His nose was stuffed up and yellow discharge was coming out so I took him into the bathroom for another steam treatment with eucalyptus oil. Every two or three hours I ran the hot water until the bathroom was thick with warm fog, sprinkled in some oil and brought the cat in to clear his nose. We sat in there for ten minutes or so. It was so hot and steamy, the walls dripped and the silver photo frame on the wall started to rust from the repeated treatments over the last three days.

Joe returned and said he would stay up with him for a while. I went to bed at eleven feeling as though I'd collapse. I fell asleep praying again for what was best for my cat.

At 12:15 a.m. Joe woke me up, "Something is wrong, he let out a really weird meow and his breathing got worse. He's panting."

In a daze, I jumped out of bed and ran into the spare room where Sprinkles was lying on the bed. Joe wanted to take him to the vet.

"No, he won't make it. He'll die in the car." I said. His eyes were glazing over and I knew this was it.

Joe was panicking, "What now, what now?" He paced back and forth in the hallway, "Maybe we should chance it and go."

"No we'll stay here. Come to the bed and pet him," I said calmly.

Joe crawled over on his knees and whispered, "Come on Sprinkles. You can do it. You can make it."

I continued petting and soothing our cat, "I love you my baby. It's OK to go now."

Joe looked over at me, a tear rolled down his cheek. I kept talking and petting. His breathing became very heavy and intermittent. He meowed a different and loud sound. He then took a really big stretch, almost like a back bend.

Joe grabbed me and said, "This is it. He's going."

I moved closer to Sprinkles' head so he could see me, he stretched out his paws toward me. I repeated "I love you" and "it's OK" over and over.

Time stood still and everything was moving in slow motion, frame by frame. The air was thick and balmy even though it was a December night. My eyes focused on him. He took a deep breath, exhaled and was gone. I saw and felt life leave his body.

"Today's the day my dad died… it's a sign… my pop's got him. He'll take good care of him," Joe sobbed.

I believed it.

It was the saddest yet most peaceful moment I'd had in my life so far. The room was filled with grace and serenity. I felt a distinct energy present that I will never forget. It was serene, harmonious, abundant, loving and nurturing.

The serenity disappeared and we were left sitting there with a dead cat and two broken hearts. We cried for hours.

I never imagined my life without him. He filled a spot in my heart that was saved just for him. What would fill that hole now?

✶✶✶

On the third day after his death, I opened the balcony door and lifted the cat coffin Joe made and brought him inside. I placed it on the hardwood floor in front of the window upstairs and sat beside him. I opened the lid and stared. My skull was an old dilapidated theater housing reels of regret and pain, showing me all those moments from the past week over and over again. I couldn't get past the guilt and couldn't accept my new situation. I lost. I never fought so hard physically and emotionally only to wind up worse off than I started. There would be no second chances, healthy to dead in three weeks and I was at fault. Either I had not done enough or I had done the wrong thing, maybe a little of both. Did he hate me now for leaving him in the animal hospital?

In my state of contrition, I could see nothing positive like I usually did and nothing meant more than saying sorry even if he couldn't hear me.

"I'm so sorry. I tried everything but it wasn't enough to save your life. I shouldn't have taken you to the Animal Emergency Clinic and left you there. You went down hill. Please forgive me," I sobbed heavily curled up on the floor next to his box. As I cried for a minute or two, my tears lessened and I inhaled deeply.

As I exhaled, I suddenly stopped. Inexplicable peace enveloped me as I sat in stillness. I sat there in a meditative state, quiet and alone, not lonely.

A few minutes later the doorbell rang. I heard the muffled voice of Joe and someone else and then silence. My head was down with my hands on the coffin looking at Sprinkles as Joe entered the room. I looked up and met his gaze. He held a huge bouquet of pink, yellow and purple flowers. He handed them over saying, "Someone is thinking of you."

I opened the small white sealed envelope and read the card, "With deepest sympathy and in loving memory of Sprinkles. ~The Animal Emergency Clinic."

I gasped, "It's a sign Joe. It's a sign! He made it, he's safe and it's all OK."

"Of course he is," Joe responded smiling.

That fragrant bouquet of life was delivered to me at the moment I needed it the most. All my doubts, anguish and guilt dissipated when I read that card. Because I don't believe in coincidence of that magnitude, the bouquet was tied together for me with a string, a string of hope that held me together too. Was it a sign of continuum? A promise of absolution? The beauty of it was that I could decide what it meant because no one could decide but me. I had control about what I wanted to believe.

There are things in my life I have no control over. But I am a do-er. I want to fix imperfect situations and help people. When there's a problem I run in with my Wonder Woman outfit and make it better. I wasn't comfortable with the feeling of permanence that death left. It's the one thing in life I could not fix and had no control over, even when I thought I did. No matter how hard I tried, I couldn't stop it and I couldn't undo it. What's meant to be is to be. For a person like me who was always searching, I wanted the answer to "Why did this happen?"

Sometimes the answer is hidden deeply in the experience and you don't find out until later.

It was both a blessing and a curse to witness a death of someone I loved. The comfort of knowing that he was not alone and I was there to witness the passing of his soul was the blessing. When I relived those painful moments in my mind, it was the curse. For a few weeks that movie of his passing played in my head over and over. It was the first time I had seen a beloved's passing and if anyone had ever asked me whether I could handle it before it happened I may have said no. I surprised myself with my own fortitude during both his sickness and his passing.

The bond I had with Joe grew even stronger. When Sprinkles died we had been married for eight years but never shared a common loss so profound to both of us. He was there for me in my darkest moments of perseverance and grief. And although he felt like he knew me before that, it solidified to him how committed I was to someone I love saying, "You never gave up on him."

Two days after the flower delivery, I was lying in bed missing him when I got an inkling to get up and go in my closet. I trusted my intuition, walked in and stood there. Something told me to come in here. It was a place where Sprinkles hid or sometimes slept when he needed R&R. He liked to be on the second shelf underneath the hanging clothes. I still had a soft fleece blanket there that I hadn't removed. With conviction, I stuck my hand inside and felt around. I touched something and pulled it out. Sitting between my thumb and index finger was one of his claws, just like the one Joe threw away.

Sprinkles' passing fueled my desire to learn more about spiritual connections, especially after the flower delivery and the appearance of the claw, two of what I considered to be metaphysical signs. I became enthralled with psychic medium John Edward when I stumbled across his show *Crossing Over*. On it he brought people messages from their deceased relatives. It had me bawling my eyes out every episode. Just like the people on the show, I wanted to feel connected to my beloved cat.

That spring I was on my way home from work one day listening to Oprah on XM. Her guest was Elizabeth Lesser, founder of the Omega Institute and author of *The Seekers Guide*. They were discussing spirituality and grief came into the conversation. Still grieving and feeling no joy in my life, I listened intently as she said, "We grieve in proportion to the love lost. Grief is like wearing a badge of how much you've loved."

As soon as she spoke the words I turned the corner and slowed down, there was a black cat, just like Sprinkles, sitting directly in front of me in the middle of the road.

Italy, Ed and a lot of Gelato

Before the death of Sprinkles, I was a happy person with sad moments. After his death, I was a sad person with happy moments.

I viewed the world in black and white and I wasn't missing the rainbows. Work was a good diversion because barely anyone knew about my cat so I could get through the day pretending all was well.

I hid my grief but then it would spring up during the most unexpected times. One evening, I was taking the train home from Manhattan. The train arrived at my stop and my chest tightened and my eyes filled with tears. I wasn't even thinking about my cat until I thought about walking in the door of my house and him not being there to greet me. I thought, don't lose it at the train station. Joe picked me up that day and I just about made it into his car when I starting bawling.

"What's wrong?" he asked. Nothing better than a greeting from a hysterical wife.

"He won't be there when I get home."

"I know." He sighed.

Wanting to overcome this feeling of despair, I read spiritual books about reincarnation, grief, continued watching John Edward on TV, spoke with other pet owners and cried.

I cried more in those six months than I had my whole life prior.

I love the quote by Maurice Freehill. "Who is more foolish, a child afraid of the dark or a man afraid of the light?"

Grief put me in that dark place but I needed to feel the sadness and come out the other end. I didn't like it but I wasn't afraid to be there for as long as it took. I instinctively knew burying my grief would be bad. That's how you get sick or mentally break down years later. I just believed what people told me, "give it time." Nothing healed me like time did.

Initially though, I behaved badly to a friend.

Suzanne and I became best friends in seventh grade. She has big blue eyes, corkscrew blond curls and a petite gymnast body making her the girl next door type, except she's talkative, comedic, raunchy at times, highly emotional and sensitive. Through the years we've only had a few fights lasting minutes to hours. We obeyed the rule of never dating the same guy, made late night excursions to dance clubs we had no business being at and shared a solid bond that will make us someday sip lemonade in our curlers on the front porch at eighty. There is gold in old friends.

My mom's memory of us in high school was a smoking curling iron which resulted in big eighties hair, big belts, big hoop earrings and big shoulder pads. That was the Friday night ritual, meeting at my house armed with a can of Super Extra Hold Aqua Net in the pink and white can, and hitting the sixteen and older club circuit. The next morning we'd wake up at eleven and get an everything bagel with bacon, egg and cheese and a Yoo-Hoo. After that we'd hit the mall's food court where we'd meet up with friends to meet boys from other towns. Dating guys from our high school was lame, in our opinion.

I adopted my BFF's Suzanne and Chrissy as my sisters growing up. The three of us lived in the same town and spent all our time together. We had a solid bond that was unbreakable. As we watched other girls backstab and fight amongst themselves, we shared secrets, built trust and loyalty within our trio.

After high school we all attended local colleges and worked part-time. Chrissy had a long-term boyfriend so Suzanne and I ventured more into the NYC club scene and went to all the places we had been dying to get into since we were sixteen -The Tunnel, Limelight, The Underground and The Palladium. Armed with fake ID, slightly smaller hair and a Long Island Railroad train ticket, we danced til our heels blistered and took the last train back home.

Now, married, mature, busier with work, our husbands and families, we always found time to spend together every few weeks or months.

When Sprinkles became sick, it happened suddenly and over the course of a few weeks. During that time I reached out and left her a message, "Hey Suzie. I hope all is well. I've been busy. My cat is very sick and I've been trying to nurse him back to health. Call me back."

She called me back a week later and left me a message, "Hey it's me. I'm so sorry it's taken me so long to get back to you. I've been so busy with the kids and their school activities. Life is crazy. Hope you guys are doing well. Call me back."

There was no mention of my cat who by this time was in his final stages of life. I was hurt but didn't have time to get back to her because I was force-feeding him and awake all hours of the night and day trying to make him well again. My life was consumed by his sickness and my emotional pain.

After Sprinkles died and I was heartbroken, high on my agenda was to lash out at Suzanne who had deserted me when I needed her the most. How insensitive. Aren't we best friends? I thought.

I sat down at my computer and wrote her an email. "Dear Suzanne, My cat has passed away after weeks of battling liver and heart problems. I am so heartbroken. I am so disappointed that you did not reach out to me during this difficult time. I thought we were friends. I guess I am only important during the fun times. Now I know better." Clicked SEND.

That evening I got home and there was a message from Suzanne that said, "Kristin, I am so sorry about your cat. I know how much you loved him, you must be crushed. I was unaware that he was sick, if you told me, I forgot. But how can you say that I don't value our friendship? I'm so disappointed and hurt that you would say that. In fact, I'm really mad about the email. Call me."

I called her back, she called me back once, I called again, but then she never called me back. She ignored my calls and emails so I stopped reaching out. Six months went by and we never spoke.

In my life the one thing I can say is that I try to be self-aware. My lashing out at her was an unexpected reaction to my devastation and grief. I was angry Sprinkles was gone and I was angry that she wasn't there for me in my time of need. I wanted her to soothe my pain, to console me in my darkest time. Feelings I had not felt before were bubbling to the surface. Shock, Denial, Anger, Sadness, Loneliness, Abandonment, Guilt, Confusion, Turmoil, Upheaval and above all Doubt. The doubt I felt about life, death, love and our connection to one another. I questioned, why are we here? To lose the people we spend our whole lives loving? How is that fair? I felt the loss of control and the safety I had always felt about life. I knew we are always changing, anyone can see that if you look at a baby but then I began to see that death changed life instantly and all you counted on vanished.

As time went by, I moved away from the anger and the situation became clearer. I could not expect her to be my savior. That was not the dynamic of our friendship, nor should it be. This was my own quest, my own wound and would ultimately be mine to heal. I had read about the stages of grief in college and now I was a real life term paper in action, moving through the emotional compass on my voyage.

And true to the book *Death and Dying*, I would also go through depression and acceptance. The acceptance part was two fold: the demise of Sprinkles and a twenty-five year friendship. I felt we'd make peace someday but now was probably not the time. She was still angry and by her own admission, stubborn.

I wrote her a letter via mail. I wrote, "I was wrong to expect you to act a certain way and to send you an angry email was a mistake. I can't blame you for being mad but I didn't think it would go on this long. For whatever reason, we needed time and you still do. I wish you love and always know that whatever happens you're important in my life and I love you."

She called me the day she got it. She was sobbing on the phone and said. "I didn't mean for it to go on like this but time flew by and it got harder and harder to reach out. I'm so glad you did. You know how stubborn I can be. You know that I love you with all my heart and that I never meant to hurt you. We have always been there for each other through the years but life has gotten so crazy lately that I honestly didn't know how sick your cat was. Had I known, I would have been there."

I have always been an upbeat person, hating to burden people with bad news or sad moods. In retrospect, how could she have known how serious it was from one message on her machine?

I did not expect the emotions that vented from my tattered heart. My normally buoyant disposition was like a sinking rowboat with missing oars. I was going down and found it hard to be lifted by anyone or anything. I just kept wishing for it all to get better somehow.

After the initial I cannot eat a thing phase, I went to insatiable sadness and I kept eating to fill the vacancy. I wanted to fill the hole with something and food felt like medicine, a caloric cure to make my senses feel good when they really didn't.

I was disgusted with myself and the way I had reacted to my grief. Lashing out at my friend, moping around, and now eating my emotions away and pretending to people that I was OK when I wasn't.

The empty hole needed to be filled but not from the outside so I put a plug in it and started filling it from within.

During this time, I found the writings of Rumi, a thirteenth century Sufi poet and mystic. I felt completely connected to his words and philosophy about life, his words either filled me with joy or moved me to tears. The beauty in his verse was timeless and found me just in time. I bought a book of his poems translated by Coleman Barks. They are daily readings. I turned to my birthday and read this:

Birdwings

Your grief for what you've lost lifts a mirror
up to where you're bravely working.
Expecting the worst, you look, and instead,
here's the joyful face you've been wanting to see.
Your hand opens and closes and opens and closes.
If it were always a fist or always stretched open,
You would be paralyzed.
Your deepest presence
is in every small contracting and expanding,
the two as beautifully balanced and coordinated
as birdwings.

This poem is my life's journey, written by a man I never knew from an Islamic country, our two worlds meshing over space and time. It's as if he knows grief is my greatest struggle and my greatest teaching. With the losses, I have won. He predicted even when I'd fall, I'd rise again. Rumi is telling me to question then to be still and listen. It's all here, this poem, my biography.

I also started a gratitude journal. Everyday I listed five things to be grateful for each day; family, friends, a hot shower, iced tea, two good legs, *Breaking Bad*, whatever. In my gratitude I knew that even the bad experiences have meaning and lessons to learn. They are the Blessons (blessing + lesson) we all experience. They are there if we look close enough. Along with the hardest lessons come the best teachers too, sometimes a family member, a friend, even a stranger.

The best teacher was my cat Sprinkles.

✶✶✶

By the end of the August, I was glad summer was over. Sad and sunshine don't mix.

"Wanna go to Italy for our tenth anniversary?" I asked Joe early in September, looking at my calendar and realizing we had nothing planned yet and it was only three weeks away. I wanted to get away, run away from the dull ache I still felt.

"Book it baby," Joe replied. And that was it; weeks later we were on a plane to Rome.

Gram was thrilled we were going there. She went there on her honeymoon with Larry, her second husband. "Oh Totie, you have to go to Venice. It's the most romantic city in the world. You and Joe will love it. I'm so happy for you." She had hoped Italy would help me bounce back from the death of Sprinkles.

Joe's mom, Joanie and her husband, Ed lived two hours away so they stayed at our house while we were in Italy to keep Lilly company and visit with friends. Joanie and Ed were married for five years. They both worked at Con-Edison twenty years earlier and met up again later through a work reunion when they both were older and single. Joanie never remarried after the death of Joe's dad when Joe was eleven. She loved her freedom to travel and socialize. Her pocket calendar had more blue ink than white paper visible due to weekends away, friendly visits and cross country trips. "I don't know how I ever had the time to work," she'd say with a giggle.

Ed was from that last generation of gentlemen who still dressed up to go to the theater or dinner. A World War II naval veteran, Ed loved to tell a joke with Canadian Club on the rocks jingling in his glass. He married Joanie knowing that life would be a social event, traveling the world with a trunk load of clothes, a paper map and a garment bar hung across the back seat. It was a long way from his solitary life in suburban New York, where his main outing for the week would be meeting the neighbors for dinner the second Tuesday of the month. He was captivated by Joanie and was thrilled to be part of her adventures.

Italy was our dream destination, and we thought what better way to cure yourself of grief and sadness but with a lot of gelato and pasta. So in an attempt to fill the emptiness, I ate my way through Italy, filling the void with cheese ravioli, pesto linguine, warm bread, Italian sparkling rose, and lots of gelato. Unbeknownst to me, there were places in Italy that housed not thirty-one flavors but one hundred flavors of gelato to meet your every need; lavender, banana, stracciatella, mint, raspberry, crème caramel and of course a good old fashioned dose of chocolate. It's amazing how much better I felt after just one week of sugar-induced euphoria.

Joe and I trekked around central and northern Italia, hitting the most succulent gelato spots in each destination. As the meters clocked on the odometer so did the kilos on the scale.

We spent the first few days in Rome, visiting the Vatican and the Acropolis. Following our *Frommers* and *Lonely Planet* guidebooks, we moved on to The Coliseum and Forum. Inside the Coliseum, I felt like I was on the *Gladiator* movie set with a dusty history, dilapidated with cracks in the walls, lopsided walkways and the smell of old dirt. Looking down from the bleachers, which seated over eight thousand Romans, I saw the center complete with trap doors and a whole underground of probable unspeakable cruelty disguised as Roman entertainment.

Just next door and stories below was the Forum, the town center of ancient Roman times where Julius Caesar reigned. Structures which dated back before the birth of Christ were still visible but gone were the people that built and actually used them, just a blip on the radar of life. Standing there listening to the history in the hot sun among the ruins made me feel small and inconsequential. For the moment I forgot my sadness and was present in the past.

Italy became a great distraction. I was so busy and mesmerized that the days flew by and before we knew it we were on a train heading to Florence, one of my favorite cities. It was the site of the Renaissance, where Europe began to move out of the Dark Ages. Everything seemed majestic and surreal. It was an artistic locale where I was surrounded by great works of art by Michelangelo, DaVinci and Raphael.

High on the list to see was the Duomo, a ginormous cathedral started in 1296, centered in a historic and bustling piazza. I sat there on the sidewalk looking up in awe, licking my gelato cone as though it was a wound being healed by history. From there, every corner I turned, was another masterpiece, another trattoria, another chance to feel like my old self.

On the last day, we crossed over Florence's most famous bridge, the Ponte Vecchio, to hike up to the Piazza de Michelangelo. I wanted to walk on that bridge because it had a great story. It was built in Roman times, destroyed by a flood, rebuilt, swept away again then rebuilt. History, drama and purpose, we can all relate to that.

The piazza overlooked the historic bridge, the Arno River and the whole city. We stood there and took pictures, held hands and smiled, hiding the scars of the past few months.

I looked down at Florence and spotted the Duomo, the Uffizi Museums and The Galleria Dell'Accademia where we had seen Michelangelo's glorious work of art, *David*. The countless cobblestone streets, gelato shops, art, cafes, piazzas, all the happy memories were starting to replace my sadness. As the blazing sun set, the fiery sky burned away my old thoughts, carrying them away like ash on a breezy day.

In the city of The Dark Ages and the Renaissance, light began to emerge and I began my rebirth.

After Florence, we drove to Tuscany, Sienna, Bellagio and San Gimignano, eating splendid pizza, gnocchi, mushroom-cheese risotto, pappardelle, and cheese cannelloni. Did I mention the pizza? We toured the wineries, the walled cities, and finally the Lake Como area, which borders Switzerland.

Our final stop before heading back to Rome to catch our flight home was Venice. I sent my mom and Gram an email with a photo of us standing at a bus stop, which is really a boat stop. The boat came and picked us up and dropped us off in different Venetian neighborhoods for cappuccinos and shopping. I scrutinized the photo, deciding my hair looked pretty good all wavy and shiny-probably from all the EVOO. And my inner light was showing through. I had a genuine smile on my face. Maybe no one else could tell but I could.

The last night we went to a concert in one of the oldest concert halls in Venice. It was the music of Vivaldi who was born in Venice. The orchestra dressed up in Baroque costumes with white wigs. They played *The Four Seasons*, which seemed appropriate in my grief evolution. Sprinkles died that dismal winter and now, entering autumn, I began to see in color again.

Back in Rome the next day, I dreamed I was roaming the halls of an ancient Italian building, searching. I was looking around corners, passing sculptures on my way. I walked into a brilliant marble room and saw my wedding dress in its pink zippered garment bag lying on the floor. I rushed to it and started to unzip it when I heard a meow. Sprinkles popped out of the garment bag and jumped into my arms. I kissed and hugged him while he nuzzled my face. It was the first dream I had had about him since his death.

I tried figuring out what the dream meant. Was it a sign from Sprinkles, an angel or a higher power telling me it was OK to move on? Or was it my own subconscious making peace with moving on? My babycat hidden away in my wedding dress, in Rome of all places, was no doubt a message to my divine self – who it was from was anyone's guess. Regardless, the sentiment was rich in the dream and when I awoke. It was if he never died, I felt his love.

Before dinner, we made our way over to St Peter's Square in Vatican City. It was brimming with people, Italians and tourists of all sorts. We had already been there earlier in our trip but wanted to go one last time since we were staying in the neighborhood.

Joe and I were holding hands, leaving the square when a black cat crossed in front of our path, stopped, looked at us and ran out of sight. It was the first black cat I'd seen the whole trip.

That paired with my dream the night before gave me hope of a mystical sort and a sense of reassurance and wonder. I ached to believe that dream was more than just a Sigmund Freud chapter telling me I was working out my neuroses. I wanted that cat in the Vatican placed there by something heavenly telling me my dream was mystical and purposeful. As I let go of my sadness, he returned to bring me joy. Or maybe he was there all along and I never realized it.

Joe and I came home five pounds heavier and a lot happier, happier than I had been in months. On the plane, I felt excited to share our travel tales and photos with my mom, Joanie, Ed and of course Gram.

We spoke to Joanie twice while we were away and she said things were fine at home. Beware of the word fine.

Joe's aunt picked us up from the airport with a smile that lasted all of ten seconds before she said, "I have some bad news." While we were in Italy enjoying ricotta bliss, Ed went into the hospital. He had been battling emphysema for the past few years and it was getting worse. During their stay he gasped for air and was rushed to the ER.

From the airport, we went directly to the hospital. My stomach sank wondering how serious it was.

We walked into the hospital room and Joanie burst into tears. She explained she was concerned about his condition because he wasn't eating that much, seemed cranky and his breathing was no better.

Each day Ed slept a lot and ate very little. Every few days, the doctor called with something else that was failing. A pacemaker was installed, then days later, round the clock oxygen. Blood tests, scopes, catheters and then a call in the middle of the night. The hospital called asking Joanie if she wanted to override the DNR Ed had signed and have him intubated with a tube of oxygen down his throat that night. Groggy, upset and recalling a talk with Ed's cardiologist that Ed would be OK she said yes to intubation, feeling there was hope according to his professional opinion.

It was a difficult decision because she wanted to give Ed every chance to live but still follow his wishes. Next came feeding tubes, more medications, and a tracheotomy. The doctors persuaded Joanie into every procedure with a promise that "this will help." Nothing did.

Ed's condition worsened over the next two weeks and our hopes diminished. We began to question the medical system. Why would they insist on all these procedures on an eighty year old man with a fatal condition? As the medical bills piled up, the cardiologist still encouraged Joanie that he could recover.

Ed spent over thirty days in the hospital suffering until the bitter end. Around five a.m., Joanie knocked on our bedroom door and whispered, "Ed passed away an hour ago." His lungs finally gave out.

We hugged her as tears rolled down her cheeks. "He's at peace now," she said.

I could not believe Ed was now gone too. Gone from the same causes as Sprinkles, heart and lungs.

The next morning we drove ninety minutes to Ed's daughter's house to break the news, Joanie wanted to do it in person. Next, the funeral home where we picked out a gunmetal gray metallic casket, wrote the obituary, picked out his suit, planned a luncheon, and arranged for a graveside naval salute. It was Funeral 101, and we were all cramming to do our best and honor Ed the best we could.

Looking back I realize more and more now there is a divine order of things. I don't think it was a coincidence that Ed was hospitalized while they were staying with us. Joanie needed us during his sickness and after his death.

It brought many sad feelings to the forefront again. My grief was now like lasagna, layered one on top of the other.

I called my mom to chat. I needed mommying. I don't know what answer I was expecting but I asked, "Why do people have to die? How am I going to do this the rest of my life?"

"I wish I could tell you it gets easier but when you love someone it doesn't," my mom sighed on the other end on the phone. "I wish I could make it better for you but I can't, just give it time."

"Maybe we die so we know how special life is," I said.

"And we can appreciate each other," she added.

Mental note: remember that when I'm annoyed with Joe after he leaves me no shampoo in the shower or toilet paper in the holder.

Ed's passing was another harsh reminder of what happens when you try and force life. In both cases, first Sprinkles, then Ed, the signs all pointed in the same direction; most of the things we did worked against them.

The Taoist concept of Wu-Wei, the action of non-action, is going with the flow and not fighting the current. When you are awakened in that sense you can respond perfectly to whatever situation arises. Acceptance would have been the better decision eventually. Because no matter what we tried, how much was spent, what we were told, we fought the current.

I don't mean that we should roll over and die with every diagnosis, but I think there comes a time when medical doctors and hospitals know the truth yet capitalize on the money they can make from continual testing and procedures, which are sometimes not related to the patients condition anyway. It's like when a heart patient is given medication that makes them constipated then the colon doctor comes in and wants to "rule out" anything else and talks the already sick patient into a colonoscopy. Sometimes it just doesn't make much sense.

I read a study from Reuters that said almost one third of Americans die in the hospital and the cost of their medical bills are $26,000 versus a discharged patient's cost of $9,000.

We as a culture need to make peace with death. Whether it is guilt, love or honor, there is a point in time where we should be making the decisions, not hospitals and doctors. I should have known better with Ed after the ordeal with my poor cat. There should have been a point where we said "Enough, let the man have some peace and dignity during his final days." There is so much emotion and stress that it is difficult to make rational decisions.

Ed's last days were arduous but I think he made it to his next life OK because he sent me a sign.

The first time Joanie and Ed had stayed at our house to watch our cats while we vacationed, they needed a lesson in door etiquette. For those of you who don't have indoor cats, rule number one, do not let them out! Vacationing owners freak out when getting a frantic call saying, "Your cat got out."

Since both our cats were indoor cats, like any concerned (or paranoid) cat mom, I made up signs on bright yellow card stock and posted them on all the doors – PLEASE CLOSE DOOR.

After Sprinkles died, Lilly was alone so I was relieved when Joanie and Ed came to stay.

Lilly had zero interest in going out, only did so once when someone left the door open and I found her cleaning her paws in the middle of our driveway. Once was enough, so we pretty much slam the door behind each guest as they leave.

Every time Joanie and Ed cat-sat, it was a running joke with Ed and the door. "Joanie, shut that door." He winked at me, showing me he was on his toes.

Two nights after Ed's passing I was sleeping when Lilly jumped onto the bed and sat on my chest. I looked at the clock – 2 a.m. "Are you kidding me? I am not feeding you now. Go away." I nudged her away.

Now if it were 6 a.m., it wouldn't be that unusual for Lilly to nag me for food but 2 a.m. was unacceptable and quite unusual.

Lilly would not quit. She touched my face with her nose over and over and when I didn't budge she stuck her back claws into my stomach as she sat on top of me. "Ow!" I knew she meant business and I finally got up. She led me down the hall, looking back as I followed her. She led me to the stairs and she continued down the steps, stopping every three, making sure I was behind her. Intrigued, I followed her down the steps when it suddenly got very cold. I reached the landing at the bottom where Lilly was sitting waiting for me. She looked in the direction of the front door. It was wide open. I gasped and I ran over and slammed it shut.

I had checked the lock before going to bed like I usually do. The door was closed and the deadbolt was set.

The next morning I told Joanie about the open door and Lilly, "Do you think that was Ed?" I asked.

Her eyes lit up, "Yes! I think he sent us a wink and a smile, courtesy of Lilly the cat," she laughed.

It was the first time I had seen a smile on her face in weeks.

That was the one and only time that door ever blew open, before or since.

Zippy Reincarnated?

Personalities are born once

A mystic many times

-From the poem; "A Light Within His Light"

by Rumi in *Bridge to the Soul*

"Is Sprinkles reincarnated as Zippy?" I asked Joe who rolled his eyes and responded, "Come on hon, that's pushing it."

I pondered this idea as I stared at my new kitty Zippy as he paced the floor waiting for Joe to finish boiling wild caught shrimp.

A few years ago I read a book called *Many Lives, Many Masters* by Brian Weiss, a true story about a Yale psychologist who counsels a patient suffering from anxiety and depression only to uncover, through hypnosis, that she's had many past lives. Under a trance, she recalls these lives and unusual facts that this average twenty year old would not normally know. She tells specific details about how to churn butter in a wooden barrel with a crank during her life in another century. In her pilot life, she recalls a specific type of aviation equipment from the 1940's and remembers being shot down and killed during an air battle in that same plane. As sessions advance, she channels spirit guides, who describe to the psychologist how the universe functions and how souls reincarnate with the same groups of souls to work through their karma. So, your brother in this life could have been your mother in another and even more freaky, your boyfriend now could have been your dad before. Eww.

My whole life I've been looking for answers to life's greatest mysteries. I'd been asked about reincarnation and whether or not I believed in it. Yes was my standard answer growing up after hearing Gram, who was my religious barometer, say, "Totie, life goes on, even after we die. Our spirits live on."

A fan of early twentieth century psychic healer Edgar Cayce, Gram believed in the so-called metaphysical world, just like I grew to. As a child, I didn't fully grasp it. I hadn't lost anyone close to me yet, so it was something I could only conceptualize on the surface. My sweet, little brain conjured up images where the departed entered through the pearly gates, which were engulfed with white airy smoke, much like at a disco. A white-bearded God, dressed in a white and silvery over-sized robe, sat on a huge marble throne and gave us our next assignment. He'd point his mystical staff toward the confused newcomer, "OK, you're going back as a snake because you lived a life of lies and betrayal," bonk them on the head and yell, "Next!"

As I got older and began soul searching, I started to ponder the concept but couldn't fathom how it all worked. Reading this book was a revelation because the author wrote it in such a way that it felt legitimate to me. The book appeared in my life exactly on schedule, as do many things during our life's journey.

I began to wonder about my past lives. One of my previous deaths may have been by knife because, on occasion, when I pick up a shiny, stainless steel blade I get an eerie, queasy feeling and sometimes I get a hard to swallow lump in my throat.

My friend went to a Past Lives Regression Specialist who recalled her former life as a medicine man in Tibet. In her fugue state, she looked down and had big manly feet. She also remembered the exact location of where she lived. Afterwards they looked up the spot on the map and there was no such place, just a big lake. Feeling certain her recollection was accurate, she looked on an old world map later. There it was, on the map, now covered by water.

So if people were reincarnated, maybe pets were too.

My first experience with death had me buried in curiosities and one I needed to excavate was reincarnation. Could that book be true? Is it possible that God is so kind as to let our loved one return in another body or reunite us in heaven or return in another life altogether to do it all over again? I wanted to believe that with all my heart. The initial research I had been doing was teaching me through others' experiences to believe in another world, that our souls went somewhere. But "the where" was the answer I needed. The sign in Italy and the flower delivery offered hope but I still craved more concrete evidence.

Dying is abstract. I think the only ones who firmly believe in ghosts are the people who see them; for others we're teetering on the border between faith and doubt.

If there is afterlife or reincarnation, and the soul continues, that means our essence is never really gone. We must be around in another form, dimension or universe. There is a theory that the body weighs twenty-one grams less immediately after death, the supposed weight of the soul.

In my quest for more answers, I went to the epicenter of Knowledge Universe, Barnes and Noble. In the section between - yes between - Religion and Philosophy was a shelf that quelled my curiosities, at least for the moment. Like little soldiers standing at attention, the books saluted me with, we are here for you girlfriend. The Dali Lama, Jack Kornfield, Thich Nhat Hahn, Lama Surya Das, and Deepak Chopra, comforted me with alternative ideas and multi-faceted approaches to spiritual beliefs, death and afterlife.

The first subject to jump out at me was Buddhism. Maybe it's my love for Richard Gere. So many choices... *Modern Buddhism, The Essence of Buddhism, Introduction to Zen Buddhism, Buddhism for Beginners* even *Buddhism for Dummies.* One explained Buddhism dates back to the life of the Buddha in Nepal and India, 566B.C. Buddhism teaches that your current life is a continuation of past life. You have one life and are reborn again and again in various forms. What you do in this life is your Karma and will dictate your next. Buddhism teaches followers a continuation of spirit and to be free of earthly attachments. The main goal is to end the cycle of rebirth and human suffering which we bring on ourselves, then you reach Nirvana.

Hmm, that sounded good but free of Earthly attachments? I wondered how that worked. Do I have to give up my iPhone?

I scanned other titles on the shelf. My fingers brushed passed books then settled on volumes about Taoism from ancient China. The Tao is considered the source of all things. In Taoism, there is no afterlife because life is life. When your physical body dies, you are changing form so there is no death. You are bouncing back to rejoin the universe in your continued life.

It sounded pain free and I'd get to see my circle of friends and family again? I liked the way that sounded, very doable.

Pulling out a red book with pretty drawings on the cover, I read about Hinduism, where meditation and yoga are practiced. Hinduism sounded the most flexible and I do love yoga and chai tea. It offers a wide spectrum of beliefs, or what some say a freedom of beliefs. Dating back thousands of years to Southeast Asia, Hindus believe in Karma, reincarnation or samsara. Hindus believe the soul is indestructible and imperishable. Death or returning to the Source is a temporary cessation of physical activity and an opportunity to re-energize and restore for the next incarnation. Although you can enjoy the pleasures of earthly existence, non-attachment is again the theme here.

Permission to enjoy earthly pleasures? Mama likey. Hmm, but there's that phrase "free of earthly attachments" again. And I'd have to work on the meditation part, my mind always wanders in Savasana– did I turn off the stove?

Books upon books, all with the common notion that death is not bad; it is part of the cycle. But the way I grew up and to many other Christians, death is viewed as sad. You'd have to wait to see them in Heaven, which sounded like some sort of fantasy world where we all played Bocce ball and tennis with wings on our back. Lately, that seemed pretty far-fetched and didn't feel grounded. I wasn't sure about the heavenly camp in the sky.

I began viewing it more as energy and formlessness. Maybe our energy is able to take on various forms whenever we wished, allowing us to still connect to our former life. A braiding of physics and metaphysical.

The true believers in afterlife such as psychics, mystics, mediums, and the like are often depicted in the news as quacks and scam artists. But this concept of ever-living souls dates back thousands of years, before the "invention" of Christianity and John Edward. The concept of no end and no beginning exhilarated me, making me even more the seeker. I selected one book on each and paid for my earthly attachments up front.

So now I was on the lookout for my cat Sprinkles, in a new body. He'd probably come back as a cat again, since he was so good at it. If God wanted us to be together again, He knows I'd look for at least a partially black male cat, since He's God and can read my mind. Of course, I never told anyone of this idea at the time. When the moment presented itself, I decided I would spring it on Joe. You are supposed to share half-baked thoughts and hare-brained schemes with your spouse.

Aside from researching, this sense of hope was one of the ways I coped after Sprinkles' death. If I thought I'd see him again, I could bear the pain of the loss at that moment. My heart was broken and I needed to believe my special cat was somewhere, waiting to return to me.

Until now, I had my memories of him that kept me going. Admittedly, Sprinkles let me dress him up in a variety of outfits, Lilly too. His last Halloween alive, I was a geisha and Joe was a ninja. As I was dressing, I put Lilly in a hula girl outfit with a grass skirt. With Lilly decked out, I put Joe's oversized bright red ninja outfit on Sprinkles and he reveled in the attention. Any other day, he would prance around his kingdom in a scarf or t-shirt of mine, dragging half of it on the floor behind him.

Each night, when I shut off the light, he jumped onto the bed next to me and put his head on the pillow and went to sleep. In the morning, if sitting on my pillow did not do the trick, he woke me up by knocking things off the night-stand or by sailing through the air onto the bed, from the six foot tall armoire, landing with a big thud. He had it down to a science.

He had nicknames like Mr. Sprinkle Dinkles, Toonsey, Mr.Mr. and Goose.

Sprinkles saw me through good and bad times for fourteen years: graduating college, falling in love, new jobs, physical injury, good dates, bad dates, my parents splitting up, my parents getting back together, moving in with Joe, getting married. His heart was full of unconditional love that showered me with affection when I came home. I was always the shiny, new penny in the room. There was no one he loved more than me. For me, that's what life is about. Love. Laughter. Joy. Sharing your heart. No matter what the source, if your heart is open, you will find love in the most unusual places.

I had him longer than I knew my husband, longer than I had some friends, my job and most certainly any other pet. When you lose a beloved pet, your home isn't the same. Each day, they are part of your world. I felt the loss in some of my most mundane moments because he was there for those too. My house felt cold, quiet and sad for a long time.

Months after he passed, a few people would hint around about getting a new cat. I had cats since birth so I knew that I would eventually get another one, yet my heart wasn't ready to open up to a new furry soul. I had my tiger-striped girlcat; Lilly and we were grieving together. I was worried about Lilly being newly alone while we worked. I knew that no new pet could ever replace Sprinkles but a friend for Lilly may stop her from the periodic crying she was doing.

Several months later in summer, curiosity got the better part of me and I started surfing pet adoption sites like Petfinder. So many cuties out there, but as quickly as I logged on, I logged off.

Then in October after Italy and while Ed was still in the hospital, my mom called me and said "Did you see *Newsday* today?"

"No Mom, I never read the paper, remember?" I pulled back my long, brown hair into a headband for the gym. News overload is too depressing and negative.

"Well, there was this little black kitten that was found in a dumpster at Home Depot and needs a home."

Intriguing. Maybe this was a sign? Maybe Sprinkles showed up by way of this little black kitten now because God saw that my interest was piquing. I toyed with the notion but was splintered. One side said, yes it must be a sign while the other said, Ed is sick, I'm heartbroken and I don't think I can commit to this right now.

Well, when you're split, you can go either way. I needed light in my life at that point. A cute little, happy kitten would be my ray of light. Besides, I'd be rescuing a cat that was dumped, maybe I could be their ray of light too. I talked myself into it, Joe agreed and I made the call.

It turned out Black & Decker, the little cat in the dumpster got adopted, but Joanne had plenty of other cats that needed homes.

"Well, I am looking for a black and white male," I told her.

I didn't want another female because Lilly was used to another male. Joanne had a few black and white females and one black male kitten, nothing that fit my criteria.

"There's no obligation, just meet them," she prodded.

"OK, come over tomorrow," and we hung up the phone.

Joanne is a vegetarian, vet tech who does a few things on the side: belly dances, trains dogs, pet-sits and rescues feral cats for adoption. I was instantly taken with her. She works all those jobs so that she can save animals. Radiating with purpose, skinny and hyper, with fluffy brown hair, Joanne found the time every day for her animals. She had a raspy voice, but when she giggled she sounded like a munchkin from Oz.

The next day Joanne came to my house with two kittens, siblings Star and Comet in a beige carrier. Star, the female, was black and white with green, mischievous eyes and Comet, the boy, was all black with big greenish-yellow eyes that were innocent and afraid. They looked like marbles and stood out against his shiny black fur. Both adorable, I couldn't choose. I didn't need to, there was no obligation to adopt but of course since I'd come this far, it meant in my heart I was ready and I could commit.

"They're both really loveable and playful," she coaxed.

I was instantly drawn to Comet, but looking at him broke my heart. Thinking about getting another all black cat, was an achy reminder of what I lost. My thoughts flip-flopped:

His eyes were pure and loving.

Maybe I should forget the whole thing.

Maybe I'll get the girl…. Lilly will be mad!

He's cute and sweet though.

I can't decide.

"Let me think about it, Joanne," I said, petting the kittens on the floor in my bathroom.

When Joanne was packing it in and ready to leave, she grabbed Comet, kissed his head and said, "Come on Goose, it's time to go."

"Did you just call Comet, um, Goose?" I asked.

"Yeah, that's my little nickname for him. I don't know where I got it from," she giggled like a Lullaby League ballerina.

Goose? I called Sprinkles Goose. Could that be the sign I was looking for? Was God saying, "Take Comet dummy. I recycled Sprinkles' soul, made him a black male, had your mother call you plus put an ad in *Newsday*! His name is Comet, sent from the heavens."

The next day I called Joanne and adopted Comet, who now calls himself Zippy.

✶✶

After a few weeks, Zippy acted as if had always lived there. Over the course of the first six months, little by little, we noticed that he started doing things similar to what Sprinkles did. He would lay in the same exact spot on the back of the chair facing the window, he'd go crazy for shrimp, nap under the dining room table during the day, even had a similar meow which sounded more like "ehhh." With every parallel, I said to Joe, "Look, isn't that weird?" He'd thoughtfully shrug, "A little." Finally I couldn't take it anymore and I said to Joe "OK, if he likes asparagus, that's it, it's him."

Sprinkles loved asparagus; it was his very favorite food. It's unusual for a cat to like vegetables, let alone asparagus. I used to make him his own special plate and one whiff later he'd ditch the catnip and come running from anywhere for this sulphur-rich, green stalk of nutrients. Joe said he liked it because it made his pee stink.

So now, for the ultimate test. If Zippy liked it too, it would be proof. There'd be no way that I'd have two asparagus loving cats who wouldn't be in someway cosmically related.

I had a one-way chat with God beforehand: OK God, if he does eat them, it's him, there's no denying it, you gave him back to me for whatever reason. Maybe it was a new experiment and you wanted to see what would happen. Maybe our bond was so strong and we loved each other so much that nothing would keep us apart, so you gave us a second chance. If he eats them, I'll believe that Zippy may be Sprinkles. Thank you. Amen.

I would make peace with whatever happened. If he ate them, it was possible. If he didn't, Zippy was still a gift from God in a slightly different package.

The Night of Asparagus was upon us. The steamer was on full blast, hissing and bubbling turning the raw, crunchy stalks into warm and tender treats. Zippy was innocently hanging around, not suspecting a thing. I debriefed Joe on the mission, upon which he replied, "This is crazy but I'm in. Let's see if the Zipster was bounced back."

Warm clouds of steamed edible shoots permeated our house. Cooked to perfection just like he had liked them before, just how he'd like them now. Am I nuts? Death has made me lose my mind. No, I was stable, just experimenting with the possibility of reincarnation. Everyone does that.

The bell on the steamer rang out, "bing!" signaling the start of my metaphysical experiment. It was the moment of truth.

Zippy had learned rather quickly that the opening of the refrigerator door equaled food, so after careful preparation and some cooling, I opened the fridge door, took the plate out and Zippy came running. I took a deep breath in and out and said to myself, to Joe and to God, "Let the truth be told."

I sat the plate down in front of him. The sliced emerald niblets awaited feasting.

We were silent. We acted casual. He sniffed. He licked. He paused. He ate. Yes, he ate. He ate the whole damn plate. Tears welled in my eyes and as Dorothy once uttered to Toto in the witch's dungeon, I whispered, "You came back, you came back." Now, because I asked God in advance for this, didn't that make it so? Wasn't it confirmation?

Joe and I looked at each other, smiling ear to ear. "That is pretty weird," Joe said, grinning, clearly amused.

"Do you think I'm crazy?" I asked Joe.

"If you are Captain of a plane full of crazy, then I'm co-pilot." We laughed.

Joe is a politics and numbers guy. He yells at the TV when the politicians are on telling us some BS. He loves to run numbers in his head to see if a business is making a profit. When we are getting ice cream he says, "What do you think this guy is makin'? Do the math. If we are spendin' seven dollaz on ice cream and that's average and he gets one hundred customers a day, times seven days, that's five grand." Then he'll figure out the rent, the cost of the cones and other expenses and estimate the profit with his eventual pretend decision of whether or not to open an ice cream parlor.

Despite that Joe seems like a black and white person, he definitely has shades of gray and a strong spiritual side. He believes anything is possible but unlike me doesn't spend hours each week thinking about the universe, quantum physics and spirituality. It is part of who I am.

My mom has said, "You've been that way for as long as I can remember. Always asking, always wondering, always deep."

Since the Night of Asparagus, I have presented Zippy with opportunity after opportunity to enjoy asparagus again, he has declined. So where does that leave me? He still does oddly unique things that are strangely similar to Mr. Sprinkles, but I will admit, I can really never know for sure. I don't think God plays sick jokes. Instead, the universe gave me hope and something to think about. Something bigger than what I can see.

And in a dark time, there was a shower of light that came from Comet, aka Zippy. There is always light if we let it in.

Sea Monkeys

The only time I can ever remember being mad at Gram involved Sea Monkeys.

It was circa 1980 and Sea Monkeys were all the rage. I wanted them bad. Along with Olivia The Stretch Octopus and Simon, a light up, musical Simon Says game. That year Santa delivered The Stretch Octopus and Einstein, the knock-off version of Simon. But I let that slide because I got my precious little Sea Monkeys too. And I didn't have to raise them in some emptied out Smucker's jelly jar because Santa brought the aquarium with the red top too. It was Park Avenue digs for the little suckers.

The real name for Sea Monkeys is brine shrimp. They came in a package of powder and when added to salt water, they came alive. They were almost microscopic when hatched but were advertised to grow really big. The commercial said so.

I was proud of my Sea Monkeys, which were growing larger by the day. I had the biggest on the block. I fed them on schedule, gave them sunshine and a warm place to live on top of my dresser. Most of my friends' died off in the early stages from neglect or little brothers but I was determined to care for mine and have them grow into cute little faces just like the box had promised.

Arriving home from school, I grabbed some Chips Ahoy cookies and headed toward my room to see my itsy-bitsy pets. Happily I skipped down the hallway and into my room, I stopped in my tracks. I scanned my white dresser, desk and hutch. My Sea Monkeys were gone. I looked in John's room, he was always teasing me, maybe he hid them. They weren't there either. I found my brother John sprawled out on the shag rug.

"Where are my Sea Monkeys?" I demanded.

He was watching *Star Trek* reruns and crunching on the latest delivery of Charles Chips.

Without glancing my way, he replied, "I don't know and I don't care. Those things are creepy."

I went downstairs to Gram's apartment to tell. She would know, Gram knew everything.

"Hi Gram, I'm home. Do you know what happened to my Sea Monkeys?"

"I flushed them down the toilet."

I froze for a second then yelled, "How could you do that Gram? They were my pets. You killed them!" I stomped my feet and waved my arms.

"I'm sorry Totie but I thought they were unsanitary," she answered sternly.

I knew that was the end of that. I was crushed. I never thought in a million years Gram would do that.

I stormed back upstairs and sulked on my bed.

My mom came home and I told her what happened.

"Mommy, Grammy flushed my Sea Monkeys down the toilet so I'm not talking to her anymore. When I ran upstairs I was crying so John sang that baby song to me about washing my hair out with bubble gum and sending it to the Navy."

I hugged her, burying my face in her nursing school uniform, feeling the scratchy white polyester next to my cheek.

She stroked my brown hair then rubbed my back in circles before she finally spoke.

"That's so sad Krissy. I can't believe Gram did that. Those were your pets and you were taking such good care of them. I will have a word with Gram and tell her not to throw out your things without permission. I'm sure Gram meant well but she made a mistake. Don't go to bed mad at Gram." She gave me a kiss and hug.

My mom always understood me. She had the perfect blend of parenting and friendship. Between mom and Gram, I was lucky to have two strong, loving women in my house as role models. They taught me values at an early age: always tell the truth, be kind, spend quality time together, love is the most important thing in your life and women can do whatever they put their minds to.

Gram had moved into an apartment in the downstairs of our house when I was about five so I really don't remember my life without her. She moved in when my parents were on the verge of divorce. My mom wanted to go to college and get her nursing degree and my dad was moving out for the first time and we needed stability. Gram sold her house and moved into ours to help my mom. This was not the first time my parents had difficulty, Gram said they always had a turbulent relationship. She told me that my mom knocked on her door a few years after getting married and Gram told her to go back home and work it out. As the years went on and the pressures of money and kids came into the picture, it got worse.

The best way I can describe their turbulent relationship is describe the way that they are opposite. Mom is an Aries homebody. She's sensitive, talkative and an only child who still relishes attention. My dad is a restless Gemini. He left home a lot to take jobs in different parts of the state as an aerospace engineer. He went where the work was in the seventies and eighties. That was when there was a huge government budget designing and building air and spacecraft. He would come back, work nearby and then find something else and leave for several months again. Not a good match for my mom, the nester.

Passion brought out the best and the worst in them. When they were apart, they missed each other. When together, they'd fight and eventually split up. It was like they loved each other deeply but were their own worst enemies and it spilled over into their relationship. It was a constant push and pull.

My parents divorced when I was six. They were on-again, off-again until I was thirty. They're off now but still friends. If my dad, John needs advice about something, my mom would be the first one he'd call. My mom is the first to call on his birthday. They are olive oil and balsamic vinegar, at times great together but also just as good on their own.

When I was growing up I wanted my parents to be a couple, for us to be a family. We were, but not a traditional one. We've had most holidays and birthdays together even when my dad lived under a separate roof. Neither ever remarried so that made it easy. As time went on, I grew used to the gravitational pull they had on one another and would consort with Gram, my sun in the crazy universe.

"Dad's moving out again Gram," I said, knowing we could have a sane conversation about it.

"I know Totie, your mom told me," she said as she patted my hand and looked at me with pools of salt water filling the corner of her eyes. "It's crazy that two people who love each other can't make it work."

"He's moving to Florida on my birthday, he said there is a job there with a five year contract and there is not much work on Long Island these days," I explained just before my eighteenth birthday.

"Don't worry Totie, he'll be back and you'll go for visits," Gram reassured.

"I'm sick of it, I hope this is the last time."

"Me too, Totie. Come on, let Gram make you a grilled cheese," she said as she lead me into her kitchen.

Like me, Gram went along for the ride with them. At times, she felt they were a mismatch and wanted my mom to start a new life. At other times she wanted us to be the perfect little family and for my parents to remain together. I always figured every mother wants a successful marriage for her only daughter, despite the reality of the situation.

I made peace with it in my twenties and rolled my eyes, "Again?" when they moved back in together. When they split again, my battle scars were like a suit of armor. I felt no pain, only annoyance. Then one day in my early thirties I had a stunning revelation - everyone on Earth is on their own journey, my parents included. I began to look at my parents as people, not solely as my parents and with that I understood that they are people that made mistakes, just like me. They are trying, just like me. They are not perfect, just like me.

Gram didn't want my mom to grow old alone. We'd had chats about it. I said, "Gram, you know that they are better off apart. They get along better that way. They're happier."

"I suppose," she said. "I guess they're two lonely souls."

During all those years of uncertainty, the one thing I knew for sure is that Gram loved me and was a person I could go to who would understand the pain I felt from my parents' splits. In Gram, I had an ally as a child and later as an adult. I always felt me and Gram were on the same team.

Many times she would end her offer of grandmotherly advice with the famous quote from the ancient Sufi writings, "This too shall pass."

She was right. After the Sea Monkey Whodunit I didn't stay mad because even at ten years old, I knew Gram would never intentionally hurt me because she loved me so much. I felt it when she smiled at me, when she sent me for tennis lessons, taught me the organ, kissed my head and even when she finished off my Sea Monkeys. She thought she was protecting me.

The next year for Christmas, I didn't ask Santa for any more toys that involved the main ingredient of scampi.

Tinkle of Dignity

We all wore *The Wizard of Oz* birthday hats on December 28, 2008 for Gram's ninety-seventh birthday party at the nursing home. I made pink champagne Mimosas and homemade cheesecake, Gram's signature recipe. She had taught me to prepare it several years before when it became too much for her to make anymore and always made me feel like I was a great baker, even though half the time it was slightly collapsed in the middle.

I gave her Charlie perfume, dark chocolate peppermint bark and a silky blue keepsake box filled with love notes. I asked everyone who was coming to write Gram a special note and put it in the box before the party, an idea I saw on *Oprah*.

She read them after the party in private and called me the next day and said, "Thank you for that Totie, it was the most thoughtful gift and I'll always treasure it"

We finished up dessert and we took some photos. I switched on the video and filmed Gram, "Any words of wisdom on your ninety-seventh?"

She forged a smile and shook her head, "Love everyone who loves you."

She paused and tears filled her eyes, and then sighed, "Ninety-seven," shaking her head again.

It was a private moment between us, no one else was watching. My eyes filled with tears behind the lens. I shut the video off and held her hand.

"You're doing great Gram." I had that weird hard-to-swallow lump in my throat.

Gram didn't have the same zest she had all the years before. She was sick with bronchitis several times that winter and her health overall was declining. She became more dependent on the nurses and confided in my mom about feeling anxious and afraid of not being able to care for herself anymore. Despite being in a long-term care facility, she still hand washed most of her garments, showered herself and buzzed around in her motorized wheelchair visiting staff, the facility's bank and Sunday mass. When she would proudly tell me of these achievements, it made me realize how much I take for granted each day. As spring approached those simple chores became a challenge.

By mid March, a week before my mom's birthday, Gram began sleeping a lot during the day. Every time I went there she was dozing off saying, "Totie, I'm so tired all the time."

She became restless at night, awakened by nightmares. Barely eaten trays of food were carted away by the orderly with an ominous look. As I sat by her bed, I wished she'd make just one joke about not eating the cruddy food and I'd run out and get whatever she wanted. But I knew it wasn't the nursing home's fault this time.

The nurses told my mom that she cried a few times and seemed frightened. She woke up screaming during a daytime nap. They prescribed an anti-anxiety pill which seemed to help her sleep peacefully. My mom asked her what was wrong and she'd shrug and fall back asleep.

A week passed and on March twenty-fourth, I baked my mom's favorite dessert for her birthday, key lime pie. We went to Gram's with low expectations of her having any birthday pie. The two days before, she had been refusing food and we had to spoon feed her or she wouldn't eat at all.

When we arrived she was sitting up in bed in a silk pink blouse and grey pants. Her hair was done and she had lipstick on.

"Happy Birthday my darling Lois." She gave us kisses and smiled, "Totie, the pie looks delicious."

Overjoyed, my mom and I spent the afternoon with Gram, talking about world politics, books we've read and my mom's new kitten, Wilbur. The nurses made us a pot of tea while we all ate the key lime pie. Gram ate a big slice and was upbeat and laughing. We had a great day and I thought Gram was better again.

We returned the next day to dashed hopes. She slept all day and never got out of bed. My mom and I went every day to spend the day with her, feeding her what she would eat or drink and hold her hand. It was surreal because we lived in a strange limbo between fear and hope. After all, she'd pulled through two times before. When she ate and drank, my hopes soared; when she didn't, I tried preparing myself for the worst. I wrestled with acceptance once again, trying to hand it to God and let go. It worked sometimes while other times I found myself crunched up in a little ball sobbing on my bed.

By day three after my mom's birthday, Gram was barely drinking anymore so she was given an IV for fluids. Next, she developed pneumonia and laryngitis. I'm a firm believer in the mind-body connection. Gram had never had laryngitis before – ever. She was barely able to speak. I think Gram got it because she didn't want to have to say goodbye. Leaving us was painful, she didn't want to go but she had to. I think it was her soul's intention.

She began moaning with pain when the nurses tried to move her. Her body was breaking down quickly. My mom called Hospice.

Hospice was an angel by way of Medicaid. I had no experience with the organization before so I assumed they just were there to administer painkillers. Aside from that, they assist patients and their families emotionally and spiritually. I had many questions and concerns. What will the morphine do? Does it speed up the process? Is she aware? And my biggest concern: I don't want her to die alone.

They arranged to come during the late evenings and early mornings when we were not there. The nurses at the nursing home are so busy and overworked that it's hard for them to spend much time with any single patient. My brother went a few times during this period in the early evenings so she would always have someone with her. They were close too but her spiral downward became increasingly more difficult for my brother to bear and he stopped coming the day after Hospice came.

I barely left her side. Gram always took care of me, now I will take care of her. I spoke quietly to her wondering if she heard me. Sometimes she would respond with a weak smile or nod, other times nothing. I told her how President Obama was doing in his first few months or who was on *Oprah*. I read her mail to her.

"Gram, you got a card from Doris, she wrote, 'wishing you well my friend, I will see you soon. Love Doris.' It's a pretty card, it has white lilies on the front." I held it up as she glanced my way and nodded quietly.

Gram asked the nursing supervisor Cathy for certain people to come to her room at three o-clock the next day. Cathy cried as she told us that Gram said goodbye to the staff at that time. She told them that it was time for her to go and that she loved them all and appreciated their hard work and care. My mom Lola and I had been so busy with all the medical decisions to try and keep her going that this news came as a revelation. She was ready and we were not.

As my mom reiterated her conversation I listened in shock. Gram said nothing of the sort to me or Lola. I couldn't respond because I didn't know how to. Gram said her goodbyes? She knows she's dying?

The struggle to make peace with her death was a daily battle for me. I wanted so much to be strong and unselfish and most of all spiritually evolved. But I couldn't escape the waves of sadness that drowned me.

The next day she was sleeping and then awoke suddenly and she asked, "Where are the cards?" It was almost as if she was dreaming of them.

"I have them here Gram, in your bottom drawer." I pointed to the oak nightstand next to her bed.

"Oh, OK," she whispered and then closed her eyes and drifted back asleep.

I knew the cards she meant. She had a bundle of cards rubber-banded together. They were special notes and greeting cards she kept throughout the years from all the people she loved. There were cards from my mom, brother, her niece and nephew, her beloved Joe and me. She had the letter I had written to her eight years ago. It was a thank you love letter. In it, I reminisced of all the special times I had with her and how much I loved her. I told her that I was grateful for our relationship because a large part of who I am I owe to her. She treasured the letter and wanted to be buried with it. I took it out of the stack in the bottom drawer, reread it and cried. I meant every word I said then and now. I kissed the letter and placed it back, fearing the day when I'd never see the letter again.

Later she awoke and I tried to give her some broth. She must have seen the pleading of my eyes because she took one sip. She still barely spoke.

The fear I carried from childhood had materialized. Gram was dying. I leaned forward and laid my forehead on her warm pink blanket on the bed next to her waist. She still smelled like Charlie perfume. I remembered our conversation a few years ago when she fell and lost her site and made me the butterfly promise. I wanted her to remember her promise to me because I was desperate, "Gram, don't forget your promise."

She looked at me blankly.

"The Butterfly." I said reaching for her hand.

She squeezed my hand and whispered, "Yes I'll remember." Then looked away, closing her eyes to sleep again.

I wished for more time. It will be so different without her, I worried, who will I be… what would I do without the love from my grandma?

I don't know why I ever thought for a minute back then that her love would die along with her.

That night while she was awake for a few moments, we cried together. Tears rolled down her cheeks as I told her, "Everything will be OK." Whatever that meant I didn't know. She responded, "We'll always be together and I will always love you."

The following day she slept all day. Sometimes she would awaken, her hazel eyes looked black and she'd just stare into air. She still coughed intermittently. I held her hand wanting to squeeze it hard and never let go but held lightly feeling her fragility through our interlocked fingers.

Teresa, from Hospice, came in to check on her. She was about forty-five with a gentle soothing voice, short blond hair requiring little attention and eyes the color of a worn out, brown leather jacket.

She patted my back reassuring, "Vivian is resting comfortably."

My voice cracked as I looked up, "Teresa, I'm so afraid she will die alone. I want to be there. But how will I know?"

She reached into her tote and pulled out a brochure about losing a loved one. I couldn't believe they had something like that.

"There will be signs to look for, the biggest one is change in breathing. Then you know it is close." She paused. "Honey, I've seen so many people pass through the years and the one thing I believe for sure is they know what they want in the end. I've seen families sit bedside around the clock, they step out for five minutes and the person passes. Or a child who lives in another state arrive an hour before they pass. If your grandma wants you to be there and share that experience, she will. If not, you have to respect that she has her reasons. Maybe she thinks it will be too painful for you and your mom. You have to accept her decision and believe me when I tell you, it is her decision to make."

Recalling all the stories I had heard over the years about people passing, I believed what she said was true. I read once that some people believe the soul in those last hours is in transition already and has the power to do exactly as Teresa explained.

My mom and I were there all day and evening on March thirtieth, I just couldn't leave. Joe and I sat by her bed. She awoke periodically, looked at us and fell back asleep. My mom went home to try and convince my brother to come and sit with us since he wasn't picking up the phone.

It was around six o'clock when Gram pointed to her side by the floor. I didn't understand what she was doing. After three failed attempts at sign language, she whispered, "bathroom." She wanted to get up. I couldn't believe it. I rang for the nurses. They offered her the bedpan but she pointed to the wheelchair. She got out of bed herself to get in. Gram hadn't done anything like that in a week. I watched from the hallway with a smile and felt optimistic. But then I caught myself and feared this was her last hoorah, the same thing I saw with Sprinkles as he jumped on the chair giving me false hope. Joy vanished with the replay of that memory. Like a flag on a pole, I was up and down, never sure I'd be at half mast.

How could I be so optimistic after what I witnessed the past few days? Gram was dying. Yet as she lowered herself into her wheelchair, my hope swelled. Her eyes beamed ahead, chin raised, spine erect and a slight upturn in the corners of her mouth, all comforting me because Gram seemed her old self in that moment.

I named Gram's last hoorah The Tinkle of Dignity. Caring for herself and being independent was Gram's mission in life. During those last few weeks when she was increasingly getting more and more dependent it became difficult for her to accept.

I called my mom at home.

"Mom," I said, "Gram got out of bed."

"What?" she said, raising her voice two octaves.

My mom raced back but Gram was already back in bed. My mom had the same mixed feelings as me, was that a good thing or a bad thing? It felt too good when I hoped it was a turnaround and like a sick joke imagining the worst. Why would God have that happen? A gift, I told myself much later. My last glimpse of Gram the way she always was, proud and self-reliant. The Tinkle of Dignity was the last time she ever got up from her bed and when she did it, she did it with pride.

After TOD, she was propped up in bed and we turned on *Dancing with the Stars*. A couple was dancing the Lindy Hop.

"Remember that dance Gram?" She nodded and watched in a trance, the same glazed look returning to her eyes.

After it was over, she whispered, "You go, go home."

My mom and I looked at each other, we couldn't. We feared leaving and her dying.

"We'll stay a little longer. You rest Mom," my mom said as she held her hand and patted her frail little fingers, still painted with faded coral nail polish.

After thirty minutes my mom leaned over to check her pulse and reassured herself, "It's still strong." Then turned to me and said, "She's sleeping now, we'll come back tomorrow."

We both leaned over the bed and kissed and hugged her. She didn't stir at all. She just lay there quietly sleeping.

"I love you Gram," I whispered in her ear. She didn't answer.

I said a prayer for Gram that night and asked God to take care of her. The clock said 11:11 p.m. I remembered a fleeting thought I'd had a few days ago but immediately buried in my psyche - Gram is going to die on Tuesday. Tonight was Monday.

The next morning at nine my mom called to say Gram made it through the night. There was no change in breathing or consciousness.

At 11:11 a.m. my mom called again.

"Gram's breathing has changed. Meet me there as soon as possible."

Love the Soul

But this love path has no expectations.
You are uneasy riding the body?
Dismount. Travel lighter.
Wings will be given.

-From the poem, "No Expectations" by Rumi

At noon I arrived at the nursing home with Joe, not sure what I would see. Hospice alerted me of labored breathing and here it was, arriving like a forecasted hurricane. I wanted to flee and not face it but I couldn't run away from her now. Instead I ran toward the epicenter while ominous thoughts swirled around me.

What would Gram look like today? Will she see me? Hear me? Will she die today? The thought of this being the last day of Gram's life was conflicting. For selfish reasons, I wanted her to live. To share my world and be a part of my life as I got older. But what life was she having in the nursing home at this point? Her body was breaking down. She had been trying to tell me that over the last few months. She'd say, "I'm so tired." I knew what she meant but brushed it off and said, "Gram, that's what happens when you get older, it's part of life." Easy for me to say.

My only comfort was that I imagined her moving on and reuniting with her family, especially her brother Percy. She wouldn't be alone then. I was hoping that Susan the psychic's prediction of her reunion with Percy would come true, but how would I know? I had only the faith in an afterlife and a "something else" that had been growing inside of me like an uncertain daffodil bulb on a warm winters day.

My mom, at Gram's bedside, looked up when I entered. Gram's breathing was rhythmic, deep and loud. Her chest moved dramatically up and down like a balloon inflating and deflating. She didn't cough once, despite having had pneumonia. Her eyes didn't light up when I walked in, they didn't even open. Without hesitation I walked over to her bed, leaned in and whispered, "Totie is here Gram and I love you."

She raised her eyebrows and moaned. The per diem nurse there on duty said, "She probably can't hear you anymore." I knew in my heart the nurse was wrong, Gram knew we were all there.

Everything looked the same in Gram's room, except Gram. The outside sun, which illuminated and warmed her room, gave life to the spring lily still sitting on her windowsill. Whiffs of Gram's Charlie perfume floated by me as I walked around the bed deciding what to do next. I watched my mom flip through her medical chart, speaking to the nursing supervisor and making sure Gram was getting whatever she needed. There would be no meltdown here - my mom took care of her mother and did what she did best all her professional years, acted as proxy for the patient in need. But as I watched my mom in action I feared the end result, a grief-stricken daughter. Gram was my mom's best friend and confidant and her life would never be the same either. I plopped down in Gram's rocker and stared at Gram for a while, trying to make peace with the sands in the hourglass.

Joe sighed and stroked her cheek with his bent index finger. Gram was the only grandma he ever knew.

Mr. Practicality finally said, "Should I go and make the arrangements?"

Joe's nervous energy took hold and he needed to be needed. He hugged me and left at one-thirty.

The local funeral parlor that we liked was right around the corner from her church. We had been there three days before when Gram went on morphine to meet the staff and ask about arrangements, just in case. Now Joe would be asking about availability for the upcoming week.

Lola and I made ourselves busy with distractions. We went through some of her drawers, compiled lists, looked at photos, read get well cards, tidied up, looked through her address book and in between my mom took her pulse. Like two book ends holding up a great novel, we sat on opposite sides of Gram in the hospital bed while the oxygen machine hissed, Gram gasped and the clock ticked.

A hospice nurse told me the last to go was hearing. We were passing things over her, saying things like, "Look at this poem, this photo of her is pretty, Gram said she liked this for the prayer card, I always loved this of Gram's."

Every once in a while I would look at her and swear she was smiling, even though she wasn't physically, I could feel it. She was smiling inside and saying, "my girls."

During that time, I was at peace sitting there with my mom and Gram, *The Three Musketeers.* This is how it began and how it shall end, I thought. Looking back, I think it was to be our fate, "all for one and one for all."

Around two-thirty I summoned my mom outside into the hall. "I think we should leave." She looked at me like I was crazy.

"Remember? Hospice said they choose when they want to go. I don't want Gram to hang on and suffer because we're here. Maybe she doesn't want us to be there when it happens. I think we should give her some space, then come back."

My mom thought for a moment and whispered back, "OK, I think that's a good idea. Let's call Doris to come over and stay while we're out. We'll leave for an hour."

We decided to say it aloud by Gram so she would know what our plan was. "Mom, want to get a bite to eat at four o'clock?" I tapped my wrist and my imaginary watch, "Doris wanted to come today and see Gram. We can call and see if she can come then."

"OK, Kristin."

We called Doris, in front of Gram, and asked her to come at four. Did Gram hear all that? Was her soul alert and responsive like I believed it was? Or was I wasting my time on actually believing her soul had a choice, like Hospice had intimated?

A little while later I found one of Gram's little pocket-sized books called *God's Minute IV*. It was 365 daily affirmations by Dr. Robert H. Schuller. She had read one every day and wrote little notes on the pages. I turned to today, March thirty-first and read: O death, where is your sting? O grave, where is your victory? Thanks be to God who gives us the victory through our Lord Jesus Christ! When the day comes that I put my feet into bed for the last time, I shall be victorious for I shall meet Your willing arms, O Lord, and hear you say, "Welcome home."

✶✶✶

Her breathing was steady and became part of the background noise; it sounded like me underwater scuba diving. It became comforting, the only thing I could rely on. At 3:15 that changed. Gram's breath became faster and faster, more intense. My mom looked up and stood over her mother and simply said, "She's going."

I got up too and stroked her arm and said, "Gram we're here. It's OK Gram."

I repeated that I loved her, over and over. I had hoped I would be strong and calm when the time came. My heart pounded in my chest and I couldn't focus on what was happening. I took a few deep breaths and grabbed my mom's hand forming a bridge over Gram's body, one of us on each side. We didn't say a word to each other but from the bridge I was looking down into a reflecting pool of water. Her eyes were a rheumy mirror image of my sad, sad eyes.

Mom stood over Gram with two fingers on her wrist and said, "I can barely get a pulse now." Her face was pale and the corners of her mouth pointed down as she said the words. I heard her say, "I love you Mama."

I kissed Gram's forehead while holding her hand, still warm. Her eyes were just barely open, the way you see someone sleep with their eyes half open. I was on her blind-eye side so I moved over to join my mom. If she could see anything at all, I wanted her to see me and my mom, next to her, all the way to the end. My hands were cold and clammy and I kept caressing her arm. My mom and I recited the only Bible prayer we knew for Gram, "The Lord's Prayer," while we stood side by side, the three of us holding hands.

The nurse on duty came in to check her pulse and heart. He made a face and said he'd be back with a little morphine in case she was in pain.

After he left I told Gram, "Gram we're all alone now. Just me and mom and you. All by ourselves. You can go now Gram, we'll be OK and we'll love you forever." We kissed her.

She took a few more breaths with long pauses in between. Then one big breath and then was gone. Within seconds, the color drained from her face and she lay there lifeless. I looked up through my tears and waved at the sky above me. Maybe she could see me, I hoped, just like the tales people tell when they come back from death. They were floating above their own body.

I grabbed her hand, it was cold. The air was dense and it felt like time stood still. I looked at the clock, it was 3:45.

Gram was free now. We were not. We sat there in shock and hugged for an undetermined amount of time. We both cried and gasped for air. We both sat down and stared at Gram. She looked completely different, just a shell, the oyster and the pearl both gone.

I looked at my wrists. There were perfectly round wet circles on my inner wrists, one on each side that seeped through my green long sleeved shirt. "Mom, look at my wrists." I held them up.

She widened her eyes but said nothing. Later we discussed it again and she said, "Stigmata."

Years of worry about her death and living without her came from a place of love and also of fear. The Stigmata sign, real or imagined, gave me comfort. For I interpreted it as God telling me she was OK and I would be too. He said, "You sacrificed your fear and comfort to help her transition into Glory. That comes from pure love."

✶✶✶

Minutes later, Joe returned and gasped.

"I can't believe she's gone," he said standing by her bedside.

Joe hugged me then told Gram he loved her and kissed her on her cheek. He was in shock and didn't expect to come back to Gram gone.

The nurse came back with the morphine. Then Doris walked in, four o'clock exactly. I felt sure that the Hospice people were right and Gram heard our whole conversation. Gram chose her passing, she wanted us there, she knew we could handle it and we wanted it too. Gram was a private person and the fact that none of her regular nurses were there that day and people weren't in and out like they usually were was a miracle in itself. She had her final moment with dignity and privacy, with her girls by her side. Exactly the way she wanted it.

Doris was upset, yet pragmatic. She had strong beliefs in afterlife, just like me and Gram.

She stayed for a while and offered me some consolation I had not expected. "Vivian is truly at peace now, she wanted this and was ready."

Gram had told Doris this over the last few weeks. "Percy knew she was coming too and –" she paused. "Wait, I'm not sure if I am supposed to tell you about that."

We shared the same beliefs too and I assured her I wanted to know everything, Gram wouldn't mind.

"Well, a few days ago, your grandma heard something while she was taking a nap during the day. She thought it was the nurse, she woke up to see what they wanted and she saw Percy standing at the foot of the bed, smiling. She felt Percy was waiting for her and felt very happy."

"Oh my God Doris, that's amazing. A psychic told me a few years ago that her brothers would be greeting her in heaven. I would have never known that, thank you for telling me."

Gram never told us about the Percy spirit appearance because she didn't want us to worry that the end was near. If we had not come up with our "four o'clock plan" and Doris had not come that day, I would not have known about Percy. A sweet, cosmic recipe, it all came together. It was my personal little angel cake.

The Blesson I learned from Sprinkles' death was to live in the present moment and savor the time left. I remembered that and put that into practice with Gram. I was able to spend that sacred time with her and just be.

Gram as I knew her was gone. I prayed for signs from her so I knew she was OK. I made a conscious decision to be fully present in the world around me so I wouldn't miss a sign if it came.

I turned to my Rumi book and read a verse from "No Expectations";

How long do you lay embracing a corpse?
Love rather the soul, which cannot be held.

Signs

I always thought I would never survive the death of Gram. Inexplicably I was still feeling connected to her; like she was still around me somehow.

During the dark days when she was dying, I imagined the scene. I'd be sitting by my pool or in a park somewhere and out of the clear blue sky, a butterfly would land on my nose. I would instantly know it was her and laugh, not for feeling silly but for her intact sense of humor in her life after life.

Imagination and reality are different, even in the metaphysical world. Gram always did things with unique style. The butterfly on the nose bit wasn't gonna cut it. She would think that was too common and maybe she was right. If it had happened that way, it may have raised some doubts.

Tonight, the night she passed, would be the first of the rest of my life without Gram. After hours and hours of crying I was laying in bed now in shock. It was as though I was floating motionless in a murky pond that was keeping me still.

I slept so deeply that night, mentally exhausted. The cats were in their usual spot, curled up by my legs and Joe was beside me. At about 5 a.m., a bright, white light flashed inside my head and jolted me out of bed. The cats were already sitting straight up like they felt it too. I sat up and instinctually said aloud, "She made it." I knew without a doubt my grandma was somewhere safe and sound and still with me. Comforted and sure, I laid back down and eventually fell back asleep.

The next morning I awoke and my thinking human brain returned to doubting the divine message I thought I had received early that morning. Maybe it was nothing, I thought, just wishful thinking and I burst into tears. I pulled myself together because there were plans to be made and a eulogy to write. I never thought before that I would be the one to give one; to have the strength to get through it. Something inside of me was ignited. I wanted to honor her in so many ways and this was one way I would do it.

After crying my way through a self-enforced breakfast, I went to my mom's house later that morning and told her about the flash of light and my hunch. "That is strange, Kristin. Maybe it was Gram."

She said it more like she was comforting me than believing in it. I told her about Gram's promise and she responded, "I hope that she does." My mom has a strong spiritual side in the way of being a good person and love and kindness is what life is all about. She doesn't go to church, never did, despite Gram's dedication to her local Episcopal church. Mom's bible is her conscience. Afterlife was a lot more to process for her than it was for me. Lola is more into The Big Bang. The idea that the Universe was created as part of an eruption of gases and matter is more believable than the Bible's Seven Day Creation. The only way for her to process afterlife is through way of physics. We are all energy and matter and the laws of physics say that energy never dies. So if I have to sell Lola by way of the atom, so be it.

Call me crazy but I was getting through the day better than I imagined, thanks to Gram. I felt her unexplainable presence and love. It still came in waves though, certainty ~ doubt ~ comfort ~ skepticism ~ belief ~...

My mom and I left her house and went to the funeral parlor, where we met Joe. We walked into the chilly lobby. It's burgundy rug, beige couches and floral papered walls were clearly trying to help you forget where you were. Bill, the funeral director was about thirty-five, handsome and sweet. He led us downstairs to pick out a casket. That room had fuzzy carpet, wooden lamps, floral walls; the look of a cozy living room. Ironic.

Caskets were stacked three high and ran the perimeter of the whole room. Dark wood, light wood, birch, oak, mahogany, pine, and the steel collection; silver, maroon, black, beige, olive. I remembered Joanie's husband, Ed's being nice as far as caskets go. He had the steel in gunmetal gray. The steel ones were less expensive unless you pick out the bottom of the barrel wood, which was not at all pretty. And you could pick from many colors. My mom liked the steel ones too and asked, "Bill, do you have anything like this green one but in a pastel color?"

Not one roll of an eye, he walked around the room pointing at three; beige, silver and light gray. Not exactly pastel. I asked, "Anything in like powder blue or dusty rose?"

He scanned a few catalogs in the office next to the casket room and called into us, "Navy blue, maroon, metallic gray?"

We walked in and shook our heads. He handed us two catalogs to look through. We handed them to Joe while we looked at liners. We were back in the casket room when we heard Joe yell, "I found it!"

We hurried back and looked down at the photo. Joe smiled, "Churchill Blue." My mom and I looked at each other, laughed and said, "That's it."

It was a beautiful steel casket in a silvery-powder blue that adorned the name of Gram's hero, Winston Churchill. Gram always knew what she wanted, even now.

I spent the rest of the day at my mom's house going through photos for a memory collage and writing the eulogy. I wanted to be near my mom, who felt the same as me. No sugarcoating our feelings. We could be real with each other, cry and even laugh at things.

Sorting thru the photos I remembered all the good times with Gram; 1981 Christmas in Florida, my surprise bridal shower, Eastertime, and playing cashier when I was little. I was obsessed with cash registers. My parents bought me a toy cash register one year for Christmas, when I was about nine. It was blue and grey with real buttons to push. When you hit CASH the drawer popped open. It had slots for money and change. Gram was the customer. I put the register at the end of the table, which acted as a conveyer belt, and she would pile up odds and ends from our house. Plates, Rubik's Cube, soup cans, a radio, a fork, Cheetos, scarves, a blender, you name it. Everything was sold at this store.

Other times, we played jewelry store. She scattered her jewelry around the kitchen and I would be the salesgirl, helping her select a sparkler and then of course ring her up on the little blue cash register. "This pearl ring will be dazzling on you. Cash or charge?"

"Cash, of course," Gram winked. Cha-ching, the drawer popped open. It came with fake money but she gave me real cash to play the game with.

"OK Gram now let's trade and I'll be the customer," I said.

I shuffled around the kitchen in Lola's high heel wedges with a sock rolled up in the back so they'd stay on and point to all the baubles I wanted – seahorse pendant, gold braided chain, hoop clip-ons, opal ring and antique cameo.

"I'll take all this and wear it right now please," I told Gram the saleslady.

"Lovely selection, that'll be ten dollars Miss," Gram's index finger was already pointed at the CASH button the register awaiting my correct payment.

Scanning the bills in my hand then tabulating in my head, I pulled the twenty out while Gram awaited my payment.

"I'll need change Ma'am," I said in my most confident grown-up voice.

Gram laughed and clapped her hands together before pushing the button sounding the register bell, popping the drawer wide open.

After selecting some photos, I made the collage then wrote the eulogy. I went home that evening, dreading the next day. I would have to face Gram lying in the Churchill Blue casket. I had anxiety seeing her that way.

The next morning, I was awakened at five a.m. again. It was the same flash that woke me up the day before. This one was bright too, but very different. It was vivid pink, purple, yellow and blue butterflies. Electric butterflies. I sat up in bed and thought, Ok, that's very clear. Then said to her with my mind, heart and soul, I know it's you, Gram. In the moment, it felt real and I believed it.

Mediums say that loved ones often come while you're asleep and you're on a different plane of consciousness. Gram knew I wasn't sure about the first flash so she tried again. Determined in life and in after-life, it's cool to think her essence remained in tact.

After I awoke, I regained the doubts I had, just like the morning before. Did I make the electric butterflies up? Even if I was asleep, it didn't feel like any sort of dream I ever had before. While doubts plagued me, hope seeped in. I was on a metaphysical seesaw, riding up and down.

After my protein shake, I wandered around my empty house feeling lonely. Grief is lonely. Joe was out with my dad. My stomach churned and I felt nauseous. I still had hours before I would leave and I needed a distraction so I turned on instant company. My rule is that I never watch TV during the day. I feel too guilty, like I should be doing something else. But I felt the urge. I flicked it on and Rachael Ray was smiling and said, "Please welcome my guest Bill O'Reilly." This was freaky because my grandma used to love Bill O'Reilly. Until he got caught not practicing what he preached. Then she hated him.

There's no real explanation of why I was compelled to watch the interview, which lasted through one commercial break. After his second segment, Rachael was wrapping it up and said, "Bill, thanks for coming on. We'll be back after the break." As soon as she uttered the words and Bill was off camera, my TV shut off *Poltergeist* style. It disappeared into a tiny little white circle in the center and then went black. My house was dead silent. I pressed the remote control. Nothing. It would not turn on and everything in the entire house was still on. It wasn't a power-outage of any sort. I sat up, looked around, the only sound was the green clock ticking on the wall.

"Gram? Is that you?" No response. "I think that was you Gram." I lay back down and stared at the white ceiling, a blank canvas to imagine anything I wanted.

I kept talking to her because I wanted to believe it and thought Gram would not want to be ignored. My heart and soul knew the truth but my brain was like, no way crazy lady. I told her today was the day and how nervous I was. I told her how much I missed and loved her but not to feel bad because I wanted her to be happy now.

Our family decided to meet at my mom's house then go over to the funeral home together. My dad drove up from New Jersey and stayed with Joe and me. That day, more than ever, I was grateful for my parents' friendship.

Bill greeted us at the funeral home, with a wince-smile combo. It was weird being altogether without Gram. Gram wasn't the fifth wheel or the spare tire in our sometimes malfunctioning family vehicle. Rather, she was an additional place setting of fine English china who added beauty, breadth and dimension to our foursome. She completed us.

Before her death, she requested a closed casket but my mom convinced her to let us open it privately. "I don't want people hovering over me, gawking," she shuddered at the thought. I looked around, the room was filled with flowers, our photos and funny knick-knacks we gave Bill: a giant Manhattan glass (her drink of choice), a giraffe statue, a Winston Churchill book and a Shakespeare bobble-head. He led us to the casket and there she was, stunningly beautiful in her light pink sparkly dress. She wore it to my wedding and wanted to be buried in it. They put some make-up on her porcelain, unwrinkled skin. Bill gave us a few minutes then came over, "I can't believe how young Vivian looks; we had to double check her date of birth." Gram probably loved that.

I kissed her cheek and held her hand. It was icy cold and rubbery. I had never touched a dead person's body before but I wasn't at all afraid like I had been at other wakes. Even though Gram was technically gone, it was still the face I knew and loved, nothing would change that. My prayer was that she was safe and most of all, happy. We gathered around the casket, bowed our heads and took a few moments to honor the matriarch of our family.

People arrived twenty minutes later. The funeral parlor gave us the smaller room, figuring she was ninety-seven. Wrong, it was standing room only. A dozen staff from the nursing home came too, some on their dinner breaks. They all told us this was the first patient wake they ever came to, "Every one of us loved her."

I read my three-page eulogy and choked back the tears so I could make it through. In it, I told funny and sad stories about her life, her family and her lust for life and learning. I also wanted people to know, "… John and I are so grateful to have our grandma this long but no matter what, it is never long enough when you love someone so much. We don't remember a time without her… And as I grew older, I appreciated her even more. She was never old to me." I closed it with a quote from a John Denver song "Perhaps Love" that Gram, mom and I all loved. "Some say love is holding on and some say, letting go. Some say love is everything, some say they don't know. But if I should live forever and all my dreams come true, my memories of love will be of you."

My mom read a beautiful poem that she had written and given Gram a few years before about being *The Three Musketeers*. My brother read a verse from the bible that Gram loved.

Toward the end of the service, I was telling my mother-in-law Joanie about Gram's vision of her brother Percy, standing at the foot of her bed just before she passed. As I finished my sentence, all the bulbs in the chandelier went dim then got very bright. Joanie looked up and smiled, "She hears you darling."

As the last people left, mom and I walked over to the casket to say goodbye. Mom took out a glass bottle from her purse, "Goodnight Mama. I love you." She sprayed Gram with Charlie perfume. "I can't believe I will bury my mother tomorrow," she wept.

I was sad for my mom. She was an only child and very close with her mom, who often told her, "I don't care if you're sixty-seven, you're still my little girl and I will always worry about you." There is no feeling like being loved by another person, at any age.

We all met the next morning for the burial and final goodbye. That was the hardest part. I hated imagining Gram going into the cold ground forever. Instead I told myself, she's not there anymore. She'd let me know that, when we were graveside, later on.

I purposely wore no eye makeup; I knew I'd look like a big raccoon by day's end anyway. I wore a black dress but threw on some red heels to honor my shoe-loving Gram. It was raining that day and my heels sunk into the mushy freshly dug dirt.

We kept the burial for close family and friends so there were less than a dozen of us standing under the drizzling skies. Her plot was under an old oak tree next to her second husband Larry whom she adored. After he passed, the plot was left to her. Her true love Joe was buried with his wife someplace else.

We each placed a pink rose on the casket then gathered around in a half circle and said a prayer aloud. As the prayer was being said, I cheated and looked around, wanting to take in the moment. The mass of black wet umbrellas glistened among the grey background. I looked down at the shiny casket with the flowers piled on top. My eyes rested past the gathering where no one was standing, just hundreds of grayish headstones, one by one. I glanced back at the one just across from hers and saw a fleeting image. Gram was twentyish with wavy brown hair and sitting on the headstone sideways, with her feet crossed and legs swinging. She was smiling at me, happy. Then it was gone.

My emptiness turned to openness. It was boundless and her energy filled me.

I closed my eyes tight, put my head down and finished praying with everyone else. My prayer was one of gratitude. Thank you God for Gram, then and now. May we always have each other in this life and the next. Amen.

Erica's Psychic Gift

One week after the funeral, cousins Jack and Erica came by the house. I hadn't seen them since the night of Gram's wake. Mourning was lonely.

Erica came in holding a big leafy green plant, more than half the size of her.

"Hey Kristin, how are you?" She hugged me and smiled. After losing her dad, she knew what I was feeling so "OK," sufficed.

"I wanted to give you something special in memory of your grandma. I was at the nursery today and found this all the way in the back. I thought you could plant it somewhere special. " She lowered down the large pot to the floor making the plant leaves sway, waving hello.

A self rated C+ in botany; I had no idea what kind of plant it was.

"It's a butterfly bush. Every time you see a butterfly, you can think of your grandma." She said.

She saw my jaw hanging open. I never told anyone except my mom and Joe about the butterfly pact I had with Gram.

"What?" she looked puzzled.

"Erica! This is so crazy! What made you pick this plant?" I gasped.

"I don't know," she paused and thought, "I just kept wandering around the nursery until I saw this. I had a feeling about this one. Why?" She gently brushed the leaves with her fingers.

I jumped up and down in disbelief. Joe and I were looking at each other laughing. Jack and Erica looked back and forth between themselves and us, clearly not in on our secret. I folded my arms and was doubled over with my head down, the way you'd stand if you felt faint. But I didn't feel that way. Tears welled in my eyes. It took me a few minutes to get the words out and explain the butterfly promise.

Gram kept her promise and delivered it in a way that I would know for sure it was she that planned it.

I felt this was even more special and real because it was from Erica. Her dad came through to me and my Gram came through to her. It was a perfectly hatched plan from our heavenly relatives.

"This makes perfect sense, Kristin" Erica said. "They're in cahoots up there." she rolled her eyes upward and pointed her finger skyward, now laughing with me.

The butterfly bush she picked grew to be five feet tall with tiny lavender flowers. Its beauty and fragrant flowers supposedly attract a variety of butterflies early summer through fall. The whole first summer and almost the entire second summer I didn't see one butterfly on the bush. Even though I got the sign I was promised by Gram, I still hoped for some actual butterfly action.

I planted it outside my sliding glass kitchen doors to the left against my house so I could easily peek every now and then.

Then one day the second summer of its life, I walked by it and saw a stunning butterfly. Its wings were cobalt blue on the inside and dark orange on the outside. It was dangling lazily on one of the lavender flowers, slowing flapping its wings, exposing their inner sapphire hue.

I ran inside and got my camera. At last, I thought, the elusive butterfly on Gram's plant!

I took several photos and downloaded them to my Mac. When I had time, I decided I would email Erica the photo with the caption saying, "First butterfly sighting." She'd love that.

A few days went by and the busy girl that I am, I forgot about the photo. When I remembered on Sunday, I decided as soon as I got home from a friend's baby shower I would send the email. I scrolled through the photos deciding which one to pick when Joe walked in the door. He was at Erica's house. He handed me something, "This is from Erica."

It was a wallet with a cobalt blue butterfly on it, just like the one on the bush and in my photo that I was sitting there uploading in my email.

Holding the wallet, still warm from the car, I felt the love.

Now as I gaze past the butterfly bush, I also see the grassy spot under the walnut tree where Sprinkles is buried. The space between the two is filled with grass. The space between the two is filled with pain. In both spaces there is growth.

The 11:11 Phenomenon

You have heard the tolling of 11 strokes. This is to remind us that with Elks, the hour of 11 has a tender significance. Wherever Elks may roam, whatever their lot in life may be, when this hour falls upon the dial of night, the great heart of Elkdom swells and throbs. It is the golden hour of recollection, the homecoming of those who wander, the mystic roll call of those who will come no more. Living or dead, Elks are never forgotten, never forsaken. Morning and noon may pass them by, the light of day sink heedlessly in the West, but ere the shadows of midnight shall fall, the chimes of memory will be pealing forth the friendly message, "To our absent members."

-"The Elks' Eleven O'clock Toast"

Gram's first husband Ben or Pop-Pop, as I knew him, was an Elk.

For as long as I can remember Pop-Pop would talk about the Elks because belonging to this fraternal organization, which started back in NYC in 1868, was a badge of honor.

Back in the day, it was considered cool to hang out at places like The Elks Lodge so Pop-Pop spent a lot of his free time there. But it was a surprise when a dozen Elks showed up at his funeral service and gave their famed eleven o'clock toast.

Pop-Pop's death was unexpected. He wasn't terminally ill. He was, in a sense, killed.

Pop-Pop was living alone in a retirement development in Pinellas Park, Florida. After his divorce from Gram in the 1940's, he married Mona in the late 1950's. They had a happy marriage until Mona died of cancer around 1970. He never married again and moved to Florida to kick back during retirement. We visited Pop-Pop in Florida and I had gotten to know him better when I lived there in sixth grade. He's the only person who ever got me to eat raw oysters with cocktail sauce and at ten years old, no less. He bribed me with his sweet smile and casual charm.

The evening of November 10, 1993, Pop-Pop went to the local Elks Lodge for a few cocktails, still enjoying nights out with his Elk cronies. He had a few too many so he left his silver 1965 Oldsmobile station wagon in the parking lot and took a cab home.

His friends recalled having a great time and he was his usual happy self, laughed at jokes and enjoyed a few cold Schlitz beers. After one or two grease monkey comments from his buddies, he looked at his fingernails and responded with a chuckle, "Changed my oil today. Sure." He always finished his sentences with a long drawn out "sure."

At eighty-five, Pop-Pop still loved to tinker around with his car. Before he went to the lodge that evening, he changed the oil and made minor repairs. His friend said he was supposed to take him back the next day to pick up his car from the lodge but he never came by.

On the afternoon of November 11th, my mom Lois received a call from a Florida hospital that Pop-Pop had passed away. Cause of death was uncertain.

My mom was heartbroken and at the same time puzzled because she had just seen him and he was fine. She ordered an autopsy.

I was in school so I stayed home with my dad while my mom and brother, John, flew down to Florida to handle the service and take care of his belongings. They said people were knocking on the door asking for things just as they arrived in his condo. "Can I have that? How much do you want for that? Let me know if you don't want that."

"They were vultures," my mom told me on the phone.

Pop-Pop wanted to be cremated so my mom arranged to have a service at a local funeral parlor. An hour into it, the Elks showed up. They were the old timers who came, gathered around and read a passage honoring Pop-Pop, their fellow and now departed Elk. At the end of it, they struck a bronze gong eleven times, the eleven o'clock toast.

Pop-Pop was healthy and fairly active. He was on meds for his low blood pressure but that was it. The morning of his death, he opened his new prescription from the pharmacy. It was the wrong medication. The pharmacist accidentally gave him medicine for high blood pressure.

It was a deadly combination for someone with low blood pressure to take pressure-lowering medicine and Pop-Pop passed away in the elevator on his way down to his friend's to pick up his car.

Lola went to court over a wrongful death suit. In the end, the courts didn't see the value of an eighty-five year old's life and she received five thousand dollars. They said his earning potential was zero and that is what monetary settlements are based on.

It was sad that Pop-Pop died accidentally instead of natural causes but when I think about it now, years later, maybe your time is your time. Quick and painless, he didn't suffer plus he partied like an eighty-five year old rock star the night before. Not too shabby.

Later when my mom was looking at the death certificate, she noticed the date and time of death, 11/11 at 11:11, the Elks sacred number.

We've always been astounded by this and it was a great story to tell but over the years the number eleven started appearing more frequently in my life.

I perceive it now as intimations from whatever or whoever is guiding me in my life.

I've presented such subject matter over various cocktails including tequila and it certainly brings about some unexpected revelations into someone else's brain portal. Slightly buzzed answers always include: angels, spirit guides, magic, God, no one – you're imagining that and the good ol' coincidence. Inebriated answers include those and some doozies like alien chip implant, signals from a twin I may have been separated at birth from and my all time favorite - the government because they put things in the water.

I feel that a universal energy force is guiding me in some unexplainable way. I call it my angels, spirit guides, God and the Universe. It's nice to think everyone has an angel rooting for them - doesn't it?

I started seeing 11:11 several years back and never traced it back to Pop-Pop until several years after Pop-Pop passed away and my mom mentioned the date he died because I forgot.

The first time I knew for sure there was something to it was the night Sprinkles died. I got a vibe that day and looked at the clock it said 11:11. Then it happened the morning of Grams death before I went to the nursing home after my moms phone call the clock said 11:11.

I had them prior to Gram's death but then after she died I had one again, this time seeming to come from Gram herself.

A few months after Gram passed I was having dinner with Joe when the phone rang.

"Your Uncle had a stroke," said Ellie, my Uncle Herbie's ladyfriend.

Uncle Herbie is my dad's older brother who looks exactly like my dad. Tall, olive skin, green eyes, high cheek bones and greyish white hair. Uncle Herbie was married to my Aunt Jean for like forty years.

After Jean died of cancer around 1990, Uncle Herbie had three or four lady friends until he found Ellie, a petite Jewish woman from Queens who loved to travel. Together they visited Antarctica, South America, California, Europe and finally Australia.

A few weeks after their return, my uncle had the stroke. Ellie found him unconscious in his bed.

After getting the call, Joe and I drove into Queens and picked Ellie up and drove to the hospital.

When I got there he was very restless and twitching a lot. His eyes were half open and he looked unconscious. I had a bad feeling about it from the moment I saw him.

I held his hand and rubbed his arm and said, "Uncle Herbie, it's Kristin and Joe. We are here now. We will take care of things. Ellie is here too. Don't worry, it's going to be OK."

My dad arrived and we spoke to the doctor who was Hindu.

"There isn't much we can do in this situation. I will keep him comfortable and we will monitor his progress. I don't recommend much more," the doctor said.

It wasn't the answer I was expecting. Where were the endless offers of surgery, of medical procedures, of brain scans? After the medical nightmare with Ed, this doctor was refreshingly honest. It was Wu-Wei again, the action of non action to the path of the predestined outcome. Or was it his Hindu culture? The doctor was at peace with the natural course of things.

I was so sad about my uncle plus still grieving for Gram. Again, I couldn't catch my breath in between deaths and I felt like I was keeping company with the Grim Reaper.

That night at home I was in the kitchen drinking some water before bed and shutting off the lights. I said aloud, please God take care of Uncle Herbie. I pray that he's not in pain. I opened the cabinet and a mesh pink butterfly fell out onto the counter in front of me. I looked at the clock and it was 11:11.

The hospital called me three hours later to tell me Uncle Herbie had passed away.

I don't have an explanation for these but I certainly don't believe it was coincidence. I never sat down purposefully at eleven o'clock and said an eleven-minute prayer.

I can tell you, with most certainty, that I do not believe in coincidences. After all, the definition of coincidence in physics is two or more signals simultaneously in a circuit. Physics is energy and energy is us. It never dies.

According to the practice of Numerology, the 11:11 sign means you are on the right track, aligned with your highest truth.

I think if we are open and aware we are always getting signs but with present day distractions, we miss them. It reminds me of a verse from the poem, "Outdoors and the Passion of the Grass" by Rumi, "And now be quiet. Very few will hear."

My husband sees the 11:11 phenomenon happening and has come to believe there is something to it too. My doubting human brain used to want to use my five senses to see things and feel things in order to believe. My heart and soul told me the contrary. The first few times it happened as a phone call from someone I was just talking about or a gut instinct I had about someone or something like a job. As time passed occurrences like my dream about Erica's dad and things like that made me sit up and take notice. The more I trusted that it was a sign from the universe, the more it happened and the more wondrous they became, especially the signs from Gram.

Remember when you were a kid and believed in the magic? Why should that change as we get older? To believe in a parallel world, another dimension or universe makes the mystery of life so compelling. If we had all the answers, life would be boring and predictable. I may never find concrete answers but I won't stop searching. The minute I do, I'm not evolving. I listen now more to my inner voice; it's the core of who I am. I choose to enjoy the enigmas and believe the mystique. Pop-Pop and Gram wouldn't want it any other way.

On the Radio

Grief from Gram's death was just as raw the following year. I found myself seeking Gram in places we loved to go, things we loved to eat and re-watching movies we both loved. Anything to feel close to her. Lola and I created a mini garden at her grave with plants she loved. Visits there were comforting but ended as soon as I got on the parkway.

In the summer of 2010, I was driving home from a week I had spent at our family's house on the eastern end of Long Island. The East End or "out east" as the locals call it, is made up of sleepy beach towns settled in the sixteen and seventeen hundreds. New Yorkers and people from all over the world go there for the beautiful beaches, wineries, farmstands and the exceptional local food.

It's one of my favorite places on Earth and I shared many happy times with Gram there.

I had a two-hour drive home and was listening to host Elizabeth Lesser on Oprah XM satellite. She hosted a show called *Soul Series*, where each week a different spiritual master or leader would offer the listener guidance and spiritual lessons. *Soul Series* gave me comfort and empathy. When I felt embarrassed about my long-standing grief a year after Gram's death I recalled it was Lesser, who said to "wear grief like a badge of honor showing how much you loved." I'm still sewing mine on with heartstrings.

She interviewed a woman who had written a book and I was soaking in every word as I drove on a long and winding road, passing scattered country stores and restaurants. Up ahead on the left I spotted a rainbow of color but didn't know what it was until I got closer. Someone had turned a closed down gas station into a makeshift art gallery. All over the outside of the building were painted metal wall hangings of various animals in vibrant colors. They reminded me of the art I often saw in the Caribbean islands.

As I passed the gas station I turned my head and looked directly at a large butterfly hanging there. It was yellow, orange, red and green. In retrospect, I thought it was weird that my eye zoned in on the butterfly despite the fifty other metallic animals hanging there. But in that moment I didn't analyze and Gram popped into my thoughts.

I felt the warmth of Gram immediately. I felt safe, loved and connected. It felt as if she hugged me.

Without thinking or censoring myself, I blurted out, "Hi Gram. I love you and I know you're here."

The radio fell silent immediately and it was quiet in my car, just the hum of the engine. Ten seconds passed and the radio came back on. The woman on the radio show said, "I love when you say that." Then silence.

"Gram!" I started laughing in the car by myself. I sensed her giggling with me, getting a kick out of surprising me like that. I felt like I could burst with joy. Gram told me she'd always be with me and love me forever. It was in the moments like these, fully present, that I believed and felt the authenticity of her promise.

I've read that it's easiest for souls to come through electronics. It has to do with the vibrational frequency.

I imagine it's similar in that you can't see radio waves but they are there, transmitting music through the air every second of every day.

It is when you turn on your radio and listen closely that you can hear every note.

Have Wings, Will Travel

A day or so before Gram passed I was sitting by her bed mourning the impending loss.

As she lay there floating in and out of a dreamlike state, I wasn't sure how much she heard in the room until I said, "Gram I'm going to miss you so much. I'll always love you. You'll always be my ever-loving Gram." That was how she signed her letters to me.

Tears rolled down her cheeks but she didn't open her eyes.

I still can't understand the complexity of accepting you're dying but not wanting to go. Her tears were watermarked with our history and our unbreakable bond designed by fate.

Every experience would be different now because Gram wouldn't be part of them. No more Friday afternoon pizza. No more birthdays for Gram on December twenty-eighth, no more lunch trips to Friendly's. No more feeling like I was wrapped in a big pink bow when I visited because that's the way Gram made me feel.

Grandmothers fill a space no one else does. They stamp our DNA and there is no erasing it. The relationship doesn't have the complexities of a parent-child relationship. It's simple and nurturing. If one is lucky enough to be a grandma or to have one, it's one of the greatest bonds.

No one else would find such joy in my travel photos and stories. Gram lived vicariously through me for the last two decades when travel was no longer possible for her. I would miss sharing my journeys with her and the message on my answering machine upon my return, "Totie, are you back yet? Call Gram as soon as you get in. I want to hear about your trip."

Despite not being able to get around much anymore, she never had a hint of resentment in her voice. She often told me, "I am happy that you are happy. You are the light of my life."

As I sat by her bedside I had the fleeting thought that maybe she can come on trips with me after she was gone as my angel. Boy, that lightening bolt did serious damage when I was young. Who thinks such thoughts? Worse, who says them?

"Gram, you'll be able to come on trips with me now. You'll see everything with me. We'll be together," I whispered in her ear, fearing the nurse would think I was a nut job.

She nodded and the corners of her mouth turned up. I rubbed her pink cheek, her skin was still so soft. She'd say it was because she never went in the sun.

Looking back, even though I didn't know it then, I was engaged in a sacred Buddhist practice that I later read about in spiritual author Thich Nhat Hanh's book, *No Fear, No Death*. He explains the vital act of sitting with a dying person and talking with them, telling stories about their life, validating their life and expressing the love you have for them. Because the dying often hang on for various reasons, it makes the transition easier for them to let go and continue onto the next phase.

I think of that time as Gram's chrysalis. She was in a state of change and transition between this life and the next. Now that she has appeared to me in the form of a butterfly, the term seems fitting.

I never knew that all over the world, butterflies are symbolic of immortality and for representing souls of the dead. Gram chose the butterfly as our allegory for her afterlife instinctually during our conversation after her accident. I'm unsure but maybe Gram knew the mythology behind these brilliantly hued flyers and loved the idea of it.

I was getting greedy but I hoped Gram would accept my invitation to travel with me, as well as show me the butterfly signs.

Two months after her death Joe and I rescheduled a vacation we had canceled while Gram was dying. We were going back to one of our favorite places in the Caribbean, Turks and Caicos. I always told Gram how beautiful the water was there, turquoise blue muddled with spheres of pale aquamarine as far as you could see. The foraging waves curled up against the sand, the result of thousands of years of crushed shells, meshing together like a lonely spinster who finally met her aging bachelor.

My excitement about going there was dampened by my grief, but I was convinced, better to sit on a beach and be sad than to be sad busting my butt at home.

The flight was early in the morning and not that crowded so Joe and I spread out for a nap during the three-hour early morning trip. Just before landing, the pilot came on and announced our descent. I rolled up my shade and looked down. Swirls of aquamarine were airbrushed onto the window like an artist's canvas. I immediately thought of Gram and began chatting to her in my head. Look Gram, see how pretty? I told you! It's so great here, you are going to love it. I'll show you everything I told you about… the giant starfish, the conch shells, my favorite restaurant and the snorkel trail in the ocean. I hope you're here with me. Can you send me a sign so that I know? Just one little sign. Then I'll know you're here for sure Gram. Love ya.

Five minutes later, we landed and Joe leaned over from across the aisle. "Look hon! I just turned on our phone and look at the screen." He flipped the phone's lit screen toward me.

The screen saver was a blue and purple butterfly. Joe didn't know I spoke to Gram five minutes before and neither of us chose the butterfly as the screen saver, it was a rented international phone.

I felt excited and validated at the same time. All my doubts over the years were becoming a thing of the past, this presence I felt coming through to me was vibrant and appeared at the most idiosyncratic times. Each time I felt stronger and more sure than ever that there is a world out there that we cannot see, smell, hear or touch but sense in our most profound selves. And in some miraculous way I was still sharing my travels with Gram, now in a completely different way.

I was also realizing that when I spoke to Gram honestly and completely from my soul, without sensor, it was then that I connected to something deeper and her spirit found me no matter where I was.

✷✷✷

Keeping busy with my daily activities and work seemed to keep my grief at bay most of the time. Then out of the blue, just like with my Sprinkles grief, something would trigger my memory and I'd be swallowed up like a cliffside house in a mudslide, sinking into Earth's depths. Some of those times, I'd go to my mom because she understood what I was feeling. Other times, I didn't want to burden her with my sadness because she was sad too and I needed to be strong for her.

Everyone told me, "Holidays are the worst."

With Thanksgiving coming up Joe suggested a warm getaway. My dad offered to rent a condo and have both our families stay in Hutchinson Island, Florida for the holiday week. Almost everyone went.

My mom and I flew down for a long weekend to meet the rest of the family, already there. We both felt happy to go but were heartbroken about Gram not being there. When we were on the plane, my mom said, "Last night I was sitting in bed watching TV when out of the blue, I smelled Cashmere Bouquet."

"That totally happened to me too a few weeks ago, except it was Charlie perfume. What did you do?" I whispered, trying to hide my surprise.

"Nothing. I just sat there and it went away. It was very weird though. It was out of nowhere," she shrugged her shoulders.

Gram's beauty regimen was simple; Vaseline, Charlie perfume and Cashmere Bouquet dusting powder. At one time, the powder was commonly found in Woolworth's and the local pharmacy but in the last decade it moved into oblivion, much like the stores that carried it.

Getting little whiffs of Gram's perfume happened to me a few times. But Lola who was ye of little faith getting them too was interesting to me.

My dad and Joe picked us up from the airport and couldn't wait to give us the condo grand tour. They showed us around the kitchen, dining room and each bedroom, explaining where everyone was sleeping.

"Where's the bathroom?" I asked.

Joe pointed to an open door down the hallway. I flicked on the light and looked around the Formica pink and blue bathroom when something caught my eye. On the counter was a bottle of Cashmere Bouquet powder. I grabbed it and ran out.

"Look Mom!" I pranced around the room, giggling, holding it up in the air.

"Oh my gosh. Would you look at that! I can't believe it." Mom's mouth dropped open.

While we laughed up a storm, everyone looked at us like we were crazy. I squeezed the bottle and a poof of white powder filled the air. The reminiscent floral smell steeped through the room and as we laughed harder, snowy particles sprinkled down, leaving evidence that Gram was here for the holiday too.

The next few days, I walked around the development every day, happy to be outside and away from November in New York. Joe, his sister Deirdre and I all rented bikes and rode through trails near the condo. Each afternoon we played tennis and swam. I kept thinking of Gram and wondered if she was here all the time with us or does she come and go. I became preoccupied with Gram's spiritual contacts. You could say it was my soul focus.

On the morning of Thanksgiving, I said a little prayer of gratitude. Thank you God for the family I have and for the family that is not here. No matter what, we have love and that is everything. I pray that Gram is safe and happy. I miss her everyday but especially on days like these.

–Amen.

I went for a walking meditation that morning. It was something new I was trying since learning about it. It is a Buddhist practice where you walk with consciousness. As you walk, you simply notice what surrounds you while you are in that moment. You don't let stressful thoughts and other distractions take pleasure away from the present moment as you walk. It teaches not to judge or label things or get caught up in, ooh I have to email so and so or yikes, my laundry is piling up. Usually I take in my surroundings: the trees, a blooming flower, a crack in the sidewalk, a bird in flight, a squirrel retrieving a nut. Other times I combine that present awareness with things I am grateful for: the shining sun, the clothes on my back, the water I am drinking, someone in my life. Mostly, I am expressing gratitude for the simpler things in life that I would normally take for granted.

Either way of practicing feels good and makes me forget all the things on my TO DO LIST.

As I walked, I noticed the blue sky with swirls of puffy cotton ball clouds. I passed a still palm tree without any wind. Pinkish flowers on a vine wrapped around a fence near someone's side gate. A calico cat sat on the grass, in a shady spot, under a large shrub. I inhaled the warm, salty air filling my lungs with life. I continued to breathe in and out, just like at yoga practice, trying not to let my mind wonder too much. The ability to do that may take years but with occasional practice I was getting better and better, especially during vacations when I was less stressed and electronically distracted. I felt the hard yet supportive concrete under my feet as I paced myself and enjoyed the journey.

I rounded the curve on the path like I had done the past few days. I followed the deep red bricks bordered with green grass. I'm so happy, I suddenly thought. Not surface happy but from a deep well inside.

I felt like someone was walking behind me so I turned around but no one was there. I stayed on my path and felt not alone. Gram? Is that you? I paused. Happy Thanksgiving Gram if you are here. In my head she responded, of course I am here. Did I imagine it? Where else would she be? I love you Gram so much and I miss you.

Something in the grass to the right caught my eye; I turned my head as I passed it to see a small marker sign posted on the grass. I kept walking. Another few steps, I stopped and turned back. I wanted to see what the sign said. I walked back ten steps. It read, THIS WAY TO THE REMEMBERANCE GARDEN with an arrow pointing right. A stone walkway led up to a gazebo. Why had I not noticed this all the other days? I followed the grey pavers leading me somewhere unknown, possibly sacred. There was not one person around as I scanned the neighborhood. I walked up three steps into a white wooden gazebo with a babbling fountain in the center, much like a Zen Garden. A sign in the middle read, GARDEN OF REMEMBERANCE. DEDICATED TO THOSE WE LOVE AND WILL ALWAYS LOVE. I looked to the right of it, there were three small round stones. On them, etched butterflies.

I wanted to shout out to the skeptics of the world and to my old self, you see? Gram is around, she loves me and she's not letting me forget that. It's true, it's really true. Love never dies. We are eternal.

Instead, I said under my breath to Gram, Happy Thanksgiving, I love you too, releasing it into the air of the Zen Garden to find her.

✶✶✶

During the months after Gram's death I learned that little things really are the big things in life you miss.

And I learned that living life would be a great healer.

So I said yes at the end of 2010 when Joe and I were invited to spend Christmas break with our friends, Brent and Mona (aka Brona) at their house in Maui, Hawaii. The Hawaiian Islands are one of the most spectacular places I have ever been. Lush foliage, plumeria fragranced air, waterfalls, looming volcanoes, shaved ices and banana bread road stops make it worth the trip.

Day one, Brona gave us the grand tour starting with the "back country" where they sell fresh, cold pineapple in little baggies and chopped coconut from little huts on the side of the road.

The next day we revved up the appetite with our first ever surfing lessons before a toes-in-the-sand Wahoo dinner and a passion fruit shaved ice for dessert.

On day three, December 28th, which was also Gram's birthday, we ventured out on The Road to Hana, the most eastern and secluded tip of Maui. Like life, the pleasure is in the journey to Hana, which is stunning. On the way, we passed rainbow eucalyptus trees, roadside waterfalls and bamboo shacks serving up homemade coconut ice cream and banana bread while our car dangled on the edges of mountains resembling huge daggers pointing to the sky.

When we arrived in Hana a few hours later, we entered a park that is on the south side of the Haleakala Volcano. In the park is The Seven Sacred Pools, a series of waterfalls that flow into natural pools below. There is also a trail that I loved when Joe and I had hiked there several years before, a four-mile round-trip hike that felt like a fairytale to me. I wanted to go on the hike again, show my friends who hadn't been yet and revisit the stunning waterfall at the hike's summit.

Lush greens surrounded our every step on the curvaceous dirt trail. As we ascended, the foliage swallowed us up and the Earth became quiet, the only sounds were our feet crushing leaves on our course. It was us and the forest, a four-mile partnership.

One third up, the trail navigated us toward a giant banyan tree. Her massive trunk sprouted branches outward in every direction, some growing back into the ground. She was like a giant wooden octopus ready to scoop me up and carry me away into the forest. Hikers gathered around her, drawn to her strength, her energy and her stillness.

We continued upward where bamboo magically appeared. At first, the bamboo was the thickness of street chalk and about ten feet high. As we climbed higher and higher, its thickness swelled, its stems lengthened. Fifty feet tall and as far as my eyes could see, we were in a city of green, surrounded by bamboo skyscrapers. We crossed dimly lit areas where the bamboo crisscrossed at their tops, creating a canopy over us. The damp, earthy air filled my lungs. I was in a fairy tale, a magical bamboo forest.

We came to a stream. "Let's cross over and up to the waterfall!" I said. I felt like a kid again, playing a backyard adventure.

"You guys go, we'll wait here," they said.

Brona was spent so Joe and I traversed the stream, river stone by river stone, making it across. When we came out of the forest, the whole Earth opened up. I looked up at the blueberry sky and heard the rush of water coming out of the mountain. Blue water vented out of a crevice, dropping hundreds of feet below, filling a pool at its base. We ran through the long unkempt grass, passing the sign that read, USE CAUTION. FALLING ROCK ZONE, toward the base of the falls. I felt like Dorothy running through the poppies toward The Emerald City. I jumped on Joe's back while another hiker took our photo.

I breathed it all in, my senses overloaded by misty air, dirty feet, sweaty clothes, earthy bouquet, outward laughter and joy within.

"It's more beautiful than I remembered," I gasped as I watched tons of water reverberating out of a crevice to the Earth below.

"Love it," Joe yelled over the rumble of water, inflecting his voice.

We watched in awe for a few minutes then decided not to keep our friends waiting too much longer. "Come on hon," Joe grabbed my hand, "they're waiting."

"Ok, one more minute, go on ahead," I shook his hand away.

I wanted one more moment in this beautiful place to say hello and happy birthday to Gram. Hi Gram. Happy Birthday. You would have been ninety-nine today, can you believe it? I heard her saying, "Perish the thought." Isn't this beautiful? I hope you are here too. I'm so thankful for you. I love and miss you.

"Kristin!" Joe was waving at me to move in his direction.

We navigated ourselves over the stream, on top of the rocks and back to Mona and Brent. We began our descent down the trail. After about five sweaty minutes, a couple stopped exactly as I was passing them and the woman said, "Look!" She bent down.

I stopped and turned around to see what they were looking at.

"What is that?" the man asked.

"A beautiful caterpillar" she answered.

On the ground in front of the three of us was a thick ivory caterpillar the size of my middle finger. She picked it up and put it in the palm of her hand while the three of us hovered over it.

"It's so pretty," I marveled over the glossy, plump larva with its tiny adorable antennae that led itself around in circles on her palm.

Brona and Joe stopped and hiked back up to me to see what I was doing. "It's a beautiful caterpillar!" I yelled over to them and rambled, "I just had a whole chat with Gram, a few minutes ago, asking for a sign and now look. Do you think it's a sign? I know it's a caterpillar but that's close to a butterfly right?"

"Yeah but look at his shirt," Brent yelled with excitement, pointing to the guy with the caterpillar standing next to me. I turned around to look at his shirt. A giant image of a butterfly filled the front of his shirt.

Knowing the story, Mona gasped, "For sure Kristin, it's definitely your grandma."

Moments like that kept assuring me that it couldn't be happenstance. It was Gram working her magic because she knew I was open and looking with my heart and my eyes. She found ways of showing me that these could not be coincidences. How much do we miss when we are not looking? Just as I may have missed the guy's shirt with the butterfly if Brent hadn't pointed it out.

I saw that event as symbolic. She knew I'd never forget her birthday and always was so grateful when her birthday was acknowledged. Why would that change now? I also think she was telling me, "Just like a caterpillar to a butterfly, I changed forms too. I am still here, Totie. Always."

Quantum Leap of Faith

Faith is my mom's middle name and I am telling you that in the literal sense. I suppose Gram named her that thinking that it's a good way to live your life. But the struggle to have my mom believe in a universal energy governed by something greater than us has been a challenge. Lola still needs science to believe in this whole communicating with the dead deal, even if it's with Gram.

Joe and I went for a long weekend to Florida for Thanksgiving with my mom. My dad invited us all down to his new snowbird condo in Florida to enjoy another turkey in the sun.

We arrived late Wednesday afternoon and on the plane ride down I had a little chat with Gram. Hi Gram, I can't believe Thanksgiving is here again, this is the third one since you're gone and I still miss you and wish you were here. Can you visit me like the last time? Please let me know that you're here with us too.

I try and not ask that of Gram too much. It seems contrived plus I am sure she is busy doing whatever angels do.

We arrived at my dad's condo, went out to eat then came back to relax and watch TV. Joe and my dad played dominos and I had total TV domination as I held the remote. I put on the digital schedule while Lola and I both scanned the blue screen looking for something we'd both like.

"How about *Restaurant Impossible*?" I asked her.

"What's that?"

"It's where this guy transforms a failing restaurant in two days and with ten grand. Most of them are complete train wrecks, it's a good show," I explained.

"Eh, sounds OK. Ooh, what about *Nova*?" Lola asked me.

"I'm not in the mood for concentrating. Come on you'll like the restaurant show," I said as I flicked to the channel and she sighed.

The host was redoing a soup kitchen. A charity makeover – double bonus.

We watched the first segment as the ninety-year-old lady who ran it cooked in a dilapidated semi-commercial kitchen where the hinges were barely working on the oven. The commercial break came.

"Switch to *Nova* for a few minutes," Lola said.

OK, I thought, *Nova* has to be better than watching blasting loud commercials for three minutes so I flicked the channel to PBS. *Nova* is an hour-long show on public television exploring different scientific topics in a simple and visual format. In other words they try and make an atom riveting. I had never watched the program before but I supposed I could tolerate three minutes.

Words like atoms, nucleus, particles, super symmetry, wormholes, blackholes and fermions were all passing between my ears testing my comprehension for tonight's topic, string theory. Lucky me.

I listened and concentrated. It went something like this.

Nova: Everything in the universe from us to buildings to gravity is made of vibrating forces of energy called strings. For years physicists believed inside atoms were indivisible particles such as protons and neutrons. String theory is showing more, it's showing tiny vibrating strings inside atoms.

Me: Oh, so there's more to an atom than we thought.

Nova: Strings are changing the way we think about space. New theories about tunnels or wormholes link distant regions of space through a tear in the universe. This goes against Einstein's laws that the universe can stretch but not rip.

Me: Hmm, I believe in universal energy and that everything is connected. I do think there's a possibility of other universes. Please go on.

Nova: When you shrink us and everything else down you have quantum mechanics or physics, which shows us that space is random and chaotic.

Me: But I disagree. I think the Universe has order, a divine order.

Nova: That's where strings come in. Strings act as a protective bubble around the tear, allowing space to rip without the chaos. The strings can move through our space into another space. This theory shows us we are surrounded by hidden dimensions and there is more than just our space. There may be entire worlds right next to us but completely invisible.

Lola to Me: That means Gram can be sitting right here next to us.

Looking at my mom with jaw open, shocked at her revelation, I just nod.

Nova: In 1995 Physicist Edward Witten explained string theory as having eleven dimensions, not less as previously thought.

Me: There's that number eleven again.

Nova: Having eleven means strings can stretch into membranes, branes for short, and with enough energy can stretch into the size of a universe. This opens up the possibility that our universe is living on a membrane that is part of a much larger higher dimensional space.

Me: Why can't we see anyone or anything else from other dimensions then?

Nova: If you are living on one brane, your atoms and particles can't get off that brane. It's as if everything were like a loaf of bread, we are just one slice. And we are stuck here because of gravity. If jelly was light and sound, it can move around the bread slice but like us it's stuck there too. But some strings or energy can move from dimension to dimension.

(Lola and I exchange lightbulb looks.)

Nova: At this very moment CERN, a lab in Switzerland is constructing the world's greatest atom smasher which hopes to show the escape of a string into another dimension as atoms collide faster than the speed of light. The proof of string theory.

Lola to Me: Yes, that should be finished in a few years. The track the atoms will travel on is sixteen miles long so it's taking a while to complete. It's gonna really be something though.

Nova: As we embark on the 21st century we embark on what may be the next layer. Ideas like string theory have opened a whole new spectrum of possible answers to age-old questions. And we've taken a dramatic leap in our quest to fully understand this elegant universe.

Nova's closing credits and music play. Then the announcer comes on and says, "Join us next time on *Nova* for "Journey of the Butterflies.""

As we watched an orange and black monarch butterfly grace the screen, flapping its wings, Lola and I both gasped.

"Oh my God. I can't believe it," Lola said really slowly.

We were silent for a few seconds then looked at each other, smiling, our eyes lit like stars in a dark universe.

"Gram is here Mom. Physics or Spirituality, no matter how you slice it, Gram is still around. She would never miss Thanksgiving with us."

"You may be right," she whispered.

Two theories and two generations, could we both be right? Is there a way to believe both and not have skeptics think I was a head wrecker? Top scientists in the physics community are embarking on new discoveries of a parallel universe and believing that there is more in existence than we can see.

I could see that it was taking Quantum Physics to have her make the leap of faith. But I decided that however Gram was coming through, we both felt it to be authentic and intelligent at the same time. Two paths leading to the same place.

And for that I was thankful.

THE Energy Never Dies

I was driving on my way home from a facial after work. The warm spring day brought out the best in me, smiling as I turned the steering wheel onto my street to see the pond. Today the pond was reflecting the twilight sky turning it into a kaleidoscope of pinks, blues and purples. The pond was the thing that sealed the deal during our hunt for a house several years before.

A lover of all things with paws or claws, there was always a natural treat for my eyes. Hopping bunnies, families of geese with their fuzzy yellow babies trailing behind them, cardinals in flight, waddling ducks, squirrels gathering their stash and other furry little things doing their thing, all living their lives.

Today was no different; a squirrel crossed the road, a small yellow bird disappeared into the branches of a tree and a lady with her dog jogged in the shoulder as I passed. Nearing my house, I saw a black lump in the road. I squinted to see what it was.

"Oh, no," I mumbled to myself as the black lump crystallized. It was a dead goose several yards away from my house, obviously hit by a car.

I pulled into my driveway and got out. As I looked in its direction, I saw another goose dragging itself with its wings, trailing two broken legs behind. I covered my face with my hands and gasped.

The goose dragged itself on the grass toward the pond but the gnarly brush between the road and the water was stopping it from getting across and into the water. It sat on the grass for a minute or two then flapped its wings trying to fly but it couldn't lift off. It flapped and flapped with all its might then sat still again. It repeated this two or three times as I watched, heartbroken.

It couldn't go any further, it was stuck.

Panicked, I ran into the house and called 911. "Hi, there is an injured goose in front of my house, can you send over some assistance?" I pleaded to the operator.

"Was it hit by a car or attacked by a dog?" she asked.

"I think it was hit because there is another dead one a few yards away," I answered as I grabbed my binoculars from the drawer.

"We'll send a police car over," she assured me.

I adjusted the focus, peered through the lenses and scanned the street to find the struggling goose in my sight. I spotted it right across the street. It hadn't moved any further toward the water. It was sitting there motionless. I contemplated what to do. Should I go over there? Should I wait for the cop and they'd take action? The Wonder Woman in me was emerging once again and wanted to save this poor bird from uncertain death.

I paced the room a few times, looking out the window for the police to arrive. What was taking so long? They said there was a car in the neighborhood. I looked through the binoculars again and saw that the goose was trying to fly again. I heard the swoosh, swoosh as it flapped its wings. They were fully extended, spanning a few feet but the goose wasn't going anywhere. I wondered, do geese need feet to fly? I kept looking through the lenses intently watching the bird. The goose began digging a hole with its wings. Scooping out the brush to form a shallow hole, it dug for a minute or so as I watched and wished the cop would come. I stared through the glass and blinked through my tears as it laid its head forward in the twigs and died.

Just like that. It had no purpose here anymore. Instinctively it knew life was over and accepted its fate. Then it departed this Earth with me as its witness.

Watching that goose, I got it. Everything came full circle for me. It was done here, no extra struggle needed. On some level it sensed that so it dug a final resting place and passed away and I was the only one to see it. I was meant to see it.

Can we see in ourselves what we see in animals? The goose that digs its own grave. The cat that runs away to die. The captive dolphin that chooses not to breathe anymore rather than swim circles in a small pool. Stories we know, stories we don't but the stories that exist in nature.

Are we the same in some respect? I've heard the stories of people on their deathbed hanging on until that certain someone comes to visit or until after the holidays. What about Gram and her passing just before my mom and I were set to leave for a while? Her goodbyes to the staff? Can we really choose at the end? Do we know and then accept while our loved ones can't?

I think the biggest difference between us and animals is our relationships. Sure some animals mate for life but most don't. All animals leave their off-spring as soon as they are capable of getting their own food, never seeing them again.

The specialness of being human lies in our lifelong bonds and love. Parent-child, husband-wife, siblings, friends, pets, we matter to others and others matter to us. Surrendering to illness and accepting their death feels like we are giving up on life and love.

Maybe people hang on for unfinished business. They are afraid to leave their partner or kids, afraid they can't make it without them. We all have our lists. Lists of places to go, chores to do, people to see, bridges to mend and scars to heal. Life isn't easy but I think that is why we are here; to grow, evolve and reach our soul's greatest potential.

I haven't met a single person who is without pain and emotional baggage. It's what we do with those challenges and those relationships that make our spirits evolve. It's what makes us different from animals.

We can learn from them too. In retrospect, Sprinkles taught me the first step about grieving and acceptance. His death was in preparation for Gram's.

✳✳✳

Two months after the goose's demise, the weather was really warming up and summer would arrive soon. Driving down my street I admired the blooming flowers and greenery bursting from the trees. A blue jay dive-bombed a grey squirrel under a tree while a kayaker floated in the backdrop on the shimmering pond.

As I approached my house I looked to my right and saw two geese waddling near the shoulder of the road. I squinted and saw behind them four little, fluffy, yellow baby geese pecking away on the grass behind their parents. Learning the ropes in Goose 101.

I remembered a few months prior the dead goose and how upset I was on that day. Now here I was smiling at these cute little lemon-colored puffballs.

On the same street a life had concluded, now a few more began. In the houses on my street, lives have ended where new ones were born. Families hurt, hearts broken then healed. Souls fully actualized, purposes fulfilled, angels created, more souls reborn.

The Energy Never Dies or The END is my concrete belief now. My journey has begun to stop looking at death as an ending and view it as a new beginning. The start of something more beautiful that we go back to. Death and grief were my biggest fears; I've let them become my greatest teachers. For as sad as I was for Gram to die, the anguish was for me but not for her. I was inexplicably happy for her just after her passing. I knew she was somewhere beautiful, peaceful, pain-free and love-abundant.

Whatever the explanation – physics or spirit - somewhere there's a space that I can't access where Gram is skipping down a shell paved path on her way to ballet class, waving to her mom and Percy who sit on green grass that smells like kiwis. Hearts grow on trees everywhere you look and our pets prance around and play. Never cold, the sun never sets yet you can always see the stars. Gram does all the things she loves and sees all the people she's missed. Free of pain, stress and worry, Gram knows that everything is how it is supposed to be right now and always will be. Her purpose there is clear, she never asks why.

And best of all, in a nano second, Gram can transport herself through the eleventh dimension to my car where she rides with me, sensed but unseen, radiating love thru her glowing energy, just before she pops over to my mom's house to watch *Jeopardy* at seven o'clock that Thursday evening.

Friday, she'll sit with and comfort an orphan child in Africa before she returns to me in New York. I'm having pizza for lunch that day and she doesn't want to be late.

The END...

Acknowledgements

Joe, I'm grateful to have found a partner who believed in the same dreams, who brings magic to my day and shares the same spiritual and human values. Together we've written one of the greatest love stories.

My mother Lois, who always told me I could do this…or anything. You gave me confidence and love. And John…I luv you both.

Thanks to my girl squad who added value to my life with laughs, tears, triumphs and fails. Chrissy, Sue, Erin, Teresa, Ellen, Tish, Brenda, Kerry, Mona, Diana and Angela, our history of real life moments is etched in my memory forever.

Joanie, you always make me feel loved and appreciated. You're my family & friend.

Early on, the encouragement and feedback from my fellow classmates at Gotham Writers Workshop in NYC was invaluable. Thanks to my then instructors Marie Carter and Kelly Caldwell for the advice that made me a better writer and for help in bringing my story to the page.

Sinead Moriarty, thank you for reading TBP and giving me support and praise. It's a wonderful and appreciated compliment coming from you, a great writer and woman.

Michael Mihaley, your talent is real. We had the same goal/dream/vision…get published. We did it. Thanks for the feedback, guidance and friendship.

Thanks to The Book Makers, namely Tracy Atkins and Tanja P. for a great design and beautiful cover.

Tony and Lytle, when I said, "I need an author photo," you came to my rescue during the pandemic and rocked it. Thanks for the beautiful photos.

My angels in heaven - Dad, Lilly, Sprinkles, Grandma Choo-choo, Uncle Herb and my Sunny, my world was sweeter with you in it. Missing you always.

My Ever-loving Gram, my kindred spirit and champion. You have to be pretty special to inspire someone to write a book about you. If I wrote 1000 pages, it wouldn't be enough to capture your magic, your spirit or your life. I am eternally grateful for your love. Until we meet again.

CPSIA information can be obtained
at www.ICGtesting.com
Printed in the USA
FSHW011508250821
84308FS